The Other Side of Ordinary

The Extraordinary True Story of One Woman's Journey Across War-Torn Europe

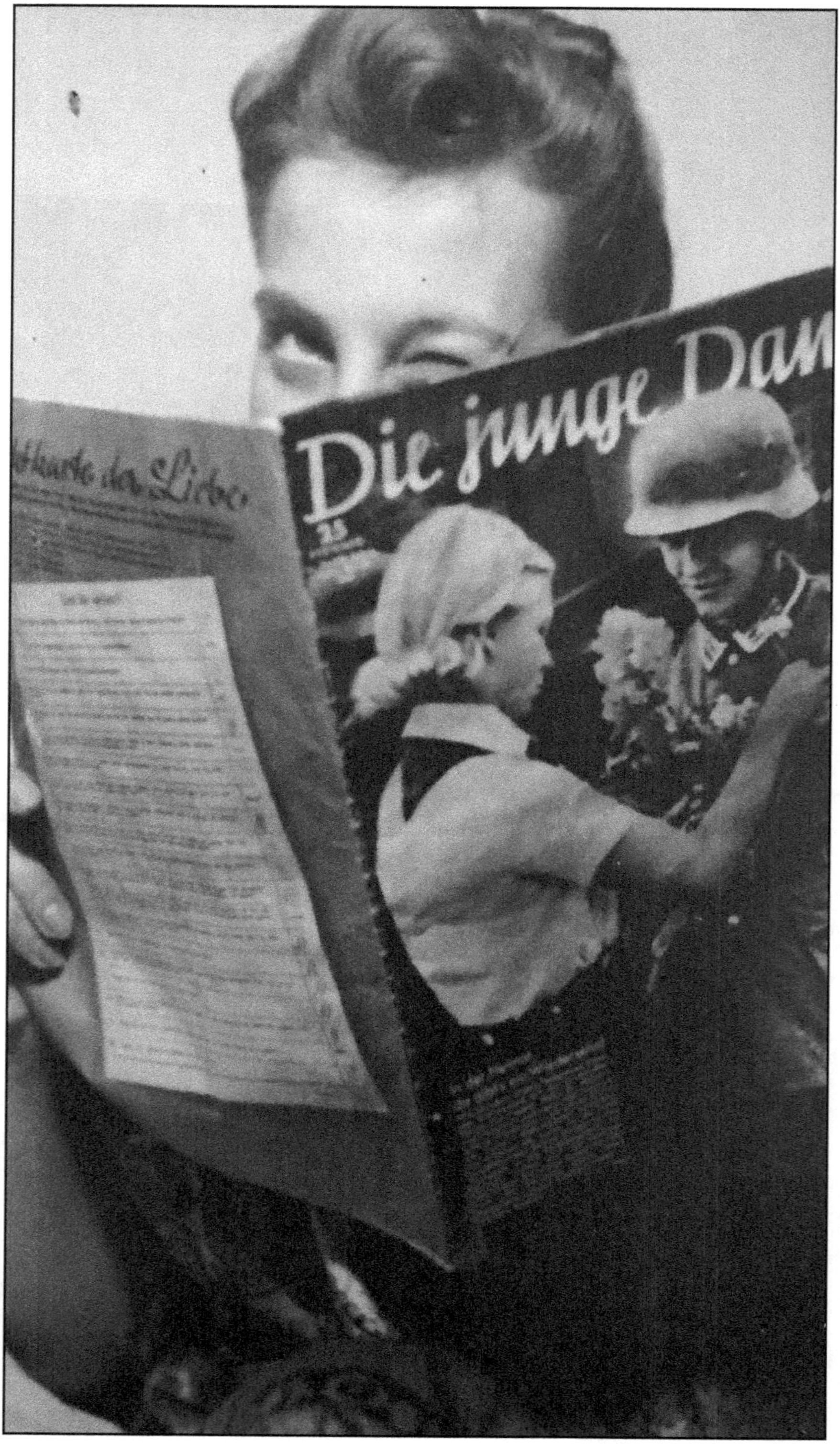
Die junge Dam

The Other Side of Ordinary

The Extraordinary True Story
of One Woman's Journey
Across War-Torn Europe

Ines Roe

Latelle Press

Latelle Press

The Other Side of Ordinary: The Extraordinary True Story of One Woman's Journey Across War-Torn Europe. Copyright © 2020 by Ines Roe. All rights reserved. No part of this book may be reproduced or transmitted in any form or by any means, electronic or mechanical, including photocopying, recording, or by any information storage and retrieval system, without permission in writing from the publisher, except by a reviewer, who may quote brief passages in review.

ISBN-13 978-0-578-23282-9

Library of Congress Control Number: 2020938142

DESIGNED & PRINTED IN THE UNITED STATES OF AMERICA

*To my mother's granddaughters
Courtney and Ashley*

Contents

Preface i
The "Ordinary" People v

Part I
The Other Side 1

1 Königsberg, East Prussia 1939 3
2 Marburg, December 1944 35
3 Marburg, May 1945 47
4 Marburg, July 1945 63
5 Marburg, July 1945 71

Part II
. . . of Ordinary 91

6 Marburg, September 1945 93
7 Paris, December 1945 99
8 Paris, 1950s 119

Epilogue 135
Acknowledgments 143
About the Author 145

We are born into a story already being told.
Our life is but the next chapter
in a tome of Living stories...
It is a story told before our birth,
throughout our life, and after we are gone.
How we live our life determines the
unfolding of this chapter and those beyond.
We hold within our power the capacity
to alter the story of our lineage.
To heal the patterns and wounds
and create a new blueprint for
future generations.

~ Julie Parker

Preface

OUR LIFE STORY IS the foundation that molds who we are. Brick by brick it becomes the structure that holds our reality. It is our "origin story." When we understand this, we can pick apart individual happenings and weave them back together to build meaning. This requires looking over our shoulder and glancing back at those who came before us. As the poem says, we are born into a story that is already being told.

The intergenerational legacy of our ancestors' lives influenced us to become who we are today. Isolated events of their lives can become touchstones of our own. Their stories help shape the arc of our existence.

Context is everything. It provides the surrounding influences, positioning an event into a bigger picture, and providing the framework that gives it meaning. It affects our interpretation of life.

Our own context helps us to understand how we fit into the world. Some say that events are just random dots floating around in our brains. Context is about connecting those dots.

Researchers in family constellation tell us that seminal events in a person's life leave DNA imprints that can transmit for three generations[1]. The implication of this research suggests that the events in our ancestors' lives can leave real-life legacies in *our* lives. There is the old saying, "The apple doesn't fall far from the tree." Understanding our own tree lets us know where we fall in the world.

Like Hansel and Gretel, our ancestors left breadcrumbs for us to follow. Our core values and principles are echoes of the past and are transmitted through our family's collective memories.

The Other Side of Ordinary is the story of my mother, Inge. She lived an extraordinary life in extraordinary times. Tom Brokaw coined the phrase *The Greatest Generation* to describe those who lived the experiences of the Great Depression and World War II. My mother was one of them, a young woman growing up in Germany in the time of Hitler. With the gift of hindsight, many of us judge those times and wonder who we might have been in that context. Thankfully, my mother was one of the lucky ones. Her experiences were not tragic like so many others but she was, nevertheless, shaped by the events of her time.

The story you are about to read is grounded in the tales I grew up with. All the people, events, items, jewelry, and situations emerged from my mother's narrative and are anchored in her life experiences. Fortunately, I did not have to trust my memory to fill in the blanks; in addition

---

1 Dias, B. G., & Ressler, K. J. (2013). Parental olfactory experience influences behavior and neural structure in subsequent generations. *Nature Neuroscience, 17*(1), 89–96. https://doi.org/10.1038/nn.3594

to having heard the stories throughout my life, I had interviews and videotapes of my mother's narrative.

Using the events of her life and viewing them as fragments of a mosaic, I was able to step back and become an observer to my mother's life. It gave me the opportunity to reflect not only on who she was, but on who I am today.

The "Ordinary" People

Inge

Henri

Moc

Inge's father

Inge's mother

Part I

The Other Side...

1

KÖNIGSBERG, EAST PRUSSIA
1939

THE ROCKING TRAIN LULLED Inge Behrendt to sleep as it lumbered through the East Prussian countryside. The last few days had exhausted her. Preparing to leave Königsberg—her family, her school friends, everything she had known—was agonizing, but she was starting a whole new adventure, like an explorer embarking on a quest, and the excitement swelled in the pit of her stomach. Nonetheless, the promise of a new chapter in her young life, and the anticipation of the journey, had taken their toll and she could no longer stay awake. Everyone's life holds juncture points that alter our path and determine our final destination, events that draw lines between the life that we knew and the life that is yet to be. Inge knew that this journey was one of those juncture points. And she was sleeping through it.

Earlier that day she stepped into the train compartment and looked at her fellow travelers, the people with whom she would share the 841 kilometers from Königsberg to Leipzig: a harried-looking mother with two unwashed children; an older gentleman, elegantly dressed, with the air of a university professor; two rowdy Wehrmacht soldiers, barely older than Inge, on their way west. How many of them were starting new adventures of their own?

She sought the most hidden seat, to be alone with her thoughts, but this was impossible. The train was nearly full, drenched in cigarette smoke and sweat, and besides, there are no hidden seats on Reichsbahn trains. Only a private compartment would grant her the solitude that she craved, but such an extravagant expense was out of the question.

"*Entschuldigung*," she said to the heavy-set man in the gray suit as she tried to squeeze by. "*Entschuldigung*" as she pushed past the stern young woman with the furrowed brow.

All of the other passengers were just as preoccupied as she was. This was fine; she didn't want to talk anyway. She was too consumed by her own thoughts for company.

She finally settled into a squeaky window seat at the rear of the train, one that gave her a last look at Königsberg and her mother waving goodbye from the platform. As the train hissed away in a plume of steam, Inge knew that her mother's tears matched her own; she could still feel the scratchy wool of her mother's coat, which she insisted upon wearing even though it was only August, as they embraced for the last time. She wanted to lose herself in that warm embrace, to hold onto it, but the future was not in Königsberg and Inge needed to let go.

Like so many of her friends, Inge had no interest in politics. Because she lived in East Prussia, away from the main part of Germany, this had been easy to do. She only heard sporadic news on the radio about what was happening, but the world was changing and events that took place in faraway places were becoming harder to ignore. She knew her mother was worried. Inge overheard the discussion with Frau Miller about the Führer's army marching into Poland, but Inge grasped only vague details of the situation and gathered that things were going well. The good news from the front couldn't hide her mother's worried look and the stress in her voice. After all, she remembered the last war and knew that dangerous times were here again.

Inge didn't want to think about any of this, but it was difficult to miss. She saw the other people on the platform. Her eye lingered on another mother saying goodbye, clutching a tall young man in a uniform who tried to fight back his tears, heartbroken by the farewell, and mounting the courage to leave.

The scene reminded her of her father. He was away, fighting for Germany, and hadn't been there to say goodbye. She remembered him making light of his military duty, sharing amusing stories with the family. Inge's favorite was about an inspection of rifles that disappeared and then mysteriously multiplied. Inge never really thought it was funny, but she appreciated his efforts to entertain her. It had been months since they heard from him; she hoped he was well. Did he know that she had decided to leave Königsberg? She had no way of knowing, but she had trusted that he would have given her his blessing. He had always encouraged her to reach for more and he wanted his only child to have what he called "an extraordinary life."

An extraordinary life was exactly what Inge wanted. She was restless, hungry for adventures and new experiences. She imagined herself assembling her life like a deck of playing cards, each card representing an episode, an event, a journey, or a person that, when spread out like a hand of solitaire, would show that she was an "interesting person."

Inge knew that this wouldn't be easy. She hadn't thought of herself as interesting. The public schools in the Third Reich groomed girls to be model Aryan women, prepared to shape their lives around the 'three Ks': *Kinder, Küche, Kirche,* or Children, Kitchen, Church. Hitler had gone so far as to issue guidelines for being an ideal woman which included not working for a living, not wearing trousers, not wearing makeup, not wearing high-heeled shoes, and not even going on slimming diets. All of this seemed ridiculous to Inge and, thankfully, to her parents too. They pulled Inge from public school early in her education and paid for her to attend private schooling. After finishing her education at the gymnasium, and passing her Abitur test, she was lucky enough to get an apprenticeship with Fritz Krauskopf, the renowned Prussian photographer. She knew that photography could be her admission ticket to the extraordinary life she craved. As a photographer there would be no limit to the people she could meet and the places she could go, and she hoped that her new life in Leipzig would hold the key.

These thoughts swirled in Inge's mind. She wanted to disconnect from her surroundings and get lost in her feelings about the future, but the stench of the engine assaulted her nostrils, and she nearly gagged when the overweight woman across from her unwrapped a greasy bratwurst slathered in sauerkraut and mustard. She peeled back her lips and took a bite, the sausage's casing snapping between her jaws. The train rocked, and Inge couldn't peel her eyes away from the brown mustard that oozed down the poor woman's blouse. After devouring this feast, she continued with a slab of apple strudel that must have weighed a full kilogram. The bratwurst had nearly made Inge sick, but the strudel was something else entirely. She had waged a lifelong battle with her sweet tooth and she envied the woman her dessert.

"Here, I will share." The woman smiled encouragingly, bits of apple and pastry clinging to her teeth, her accent broadcasting to all that she hailed from Bavaria. "Do you want a taste? My mother baked it yesterday, and it is delicious."

Inge could almost taste the tart, sugary fruit, but a bite of the strudel might come with the unwanted baggage of an hours-long conversation that she would rather avoid. "No, thank you," she said unconvincingly. But she still couldn't help looking.

To distract herself, Inge rummaged in her black purse and found what she was looking for: a small gold and silver mirror her mother had given her at the station. It was her goodbye gift, given so that, as her mother said, "You will always remember us and your ancestors in East Prussia." She looked into the glass and met her own gaze. Her green eyes were puffy from crying. Inge never allowed herself to cry, but today's sadness and excitement was an exception. She had allowed herself to cry, just this once.

She thought her long, straight nose was sharp and imposing, but it was her father's nose and this pleased her. Her lips were full and, today, they were painted bright red. Just above her lips, on the left side, was a distinction that Inge thought gave her face character: a mole that she accentuated each day with a black makeup pencil which she also used to tint her brows. Inge had the unique talent of raising one single eyebrow. This gesture was a powerful statement. With one raised brow, Inge cóuld communicate an edginess that she liked to think set her apart from the other girls. She rehearsed it in the mirror, making sure to get it just right.

She cocked her head this way and that to check her ears. Like her nose, they were too large for her face, so she had learned to strategically comb her wavy brown hair around them to create the illusion that they were smaller than they actually were. All in all, she liked what she saw.

Was she too vain? She toyed with the idea. She did like to spend hours scouring fashion magazines, looking for ways to be more elegant. Her favorite was *Die Junge Dame* and, at eighteen years old, she was a *Junge Dame*, a young woman, and she wanted to look like the models in the magazine. She was enchanted by fashion and American movies. To the disapproval of her mother, she listened to hours of Benny Goodman and would sneak out to the cinema to watch Fred Astaire and Ginger Rogers dance across the screen.

The train lurched, waking Inge from a deep sleep. The next stop was Leipzig, and they were already slowing down. Inge's stomach turned. A new life awaited outside. Frau Epler, an old widowed acquaintance of her mother's, had agreed to meet her at the station and give her room and board until she could get on her feet. When the train expelled its last puff of smoke she gathered her small brown suitcase, pressed her black hat on her head, and armed herself with confidence. She stepped down to the platform and searched the faces of the crowd.

She spotted Frau Epler. Inge had forgotten the first impression she had made years ago in Königsberg, but seeing her today brought it all back. Her pinched, feline face shot a chill through Inge's bones. Her small eyes were too close together and squinted upwards; gray hair pulled into a severe bun amplified her angular, bony features. Inge felt a thickness in her throat, and a foreboding.

She reminded herself that Frau Epler offered her a home while she studied at the Photography Institute. She should be grateful. She pasted on a big smile and curtsied the way she had been taught. Should she give the customary *Heil Hitler* greeting? She decided against it.

"Hello, Frau Epler. It is so generous of you to meet me. I am thankful for your kindness."

Frau Epler only grunted. Inge wondered why she had offered the hospitality. She didn't seem pleased to see her, and simply turned on her heel and stalked away, expecting her to follow.

Inge pressed through the crowd and hurried to keep up. She looked at her shoes and was sorry she had worn her new brown pumps; they were dusty and scuffed from all the activity in the station. Plus, they made it hard to move fast. She wanted to look around and take in her new surroundings, but Frau Epler did not have the patience for such an indulgence. She was a woman on a mission, and Inge sensed that she was an inconvenience, interrupting some other single-minded purpose.

As they left the station Inge got her first view of Leipzig. She thought she was accustomed to life in a big city, but Leipzig made her feel small. The broad, tree-lined street brimmed with pedestrians and whirling bicyclists. She was captivated by the cacophony of the passing cars and the massive military vehicles crisscrossing the avenues. The crowds and the tumult were overwhelming, and she felt the bile rise in her stomach. *Had she made a mistake?*

Frau Epler's driver pulled up to the sidewalk, and they stepped into the back seat. Inge sat stiffly next to her hostess and smiled at the driver. "What a wonderful Autumn day," she said. Frau Epler only nodded. Inge badly needed comfort and reassurance, but Frau Epler offered only the aroma of boiled cabbage that seemed to have seeped into her clothing and skin. After a long awkward pause, the car parked in front of an old stuccoed house that Inge assumed would be her new home.

Inge clutched her suitcase and followed Frau Epler through the door into what seemed like another century. The parlor was filled with ponderous ornate furniture that reminded her of photos of her grandparents' home, the walls were covered with pea-green paper, and the windows were draped in heavy flowered curtains that left the room in a haze, with dust particles floating in the space before her eyes, twinkling in the dimmed sunlight. The musty smell of ancient upholstery filled her nostrils. Despite the lavish show, Inge saw the tattered, well-worn sofa and the threadbare carpet. She smelled the mildew that wafted from the dripping faucet in the kitchen.

Inge followed Frau Epler up the narrow stairs to the third floor, the boards creaking beneath her feet. They stopped at a tiny dark bedroom, and Frau Epler spoke her first words. "This will be your quarters," she said. In the corner was a small bed with a thin mattress. Her mind flashed back to her warm, cozy bedroom in Königsberg. She felt her stomach quiver and tears pool in her eyes.

Frau Epler continued, "I expect you will be home each night at seven and lights out by nine. I will not put up with late-night partying or carousing. No phonograph or radio. No food in your room. No boys. Your door will be open when you have company. I will not tolerate hussies or hooligans in my home. I expect you to be clean and quiet. Your bed is to be made, your clothing folded or hung, and your floor swept every day. I am letting you stay here as a favor to your mother, and I do not expect to be disturbed. You are to be invisible and silent. Is that understood?"

"I do." Inge's mother trusted Inge and had given her a great deal of freedom. She had good times with friends, visiting coffee houses, and going to the late movies. This harsh new life in Frau Epler's house would be a terrible adjustment. Inge thought, *I am growing up and need to take life more seriously,* but she knew she would not last long living there.

Faru Epler said, "Be down for dinner at six."

Inge fought back the tears and responded, "I will. Thank you."

She sat on the narrow mattress and contemplated her surroundings. This is not how she imagined her new life would start. Gratitude felt like the appropriate emotion, but Inge only felt regret. When she placed the photo of her smiling parents on the nightstand, the homesickness grew in her chest and climbed into her throat.

Frau Epler served a spartan supper of flavorless boiled beef and potatoes. Inge took a bite of watery meat. "Thank you, Frau Epler. This is delicious." Her hostess stopped chewing and eyed Inge with stony silence for a moment, then turned her eyes back to her plate.

They ate in awkward silence for a few minutes. Finally, Frau Epler said, "When are you leaving?"

Inge's mouth hung open in astonishment. "I only just arrived."

She repeated the question. *"When are you leaving?"*

Inge's eyes narrowed. She fished a strand of beef from between her teeth with her tongue. "I will leave as soon as I am able."

Inge climbed the stairs to her room. As she prepared her clothes for her first day at the Photography Institute she imagined writing to her mother to tell her how much she missed her. But she wouldn't do that. Not yet. She couldn't let her know that she felt any uncertainty. She had made the decision to come to Leipzig. She would persevere and succeed.

The next morning Inge woke to the warmth of the sun streaming through the dirty windows. The sunlight repaired her hope, and a fresh resolve descended. This room, and Frau Epler's hospitality, were not what this journey was about. This was only a way station to a brighter tomorrow that she knew awaited her in the coming weeks and months. Her excitement returned, and she was ready to start a new day.

Inge wondered what type of photographs she would be working on at the institute. When she worked for Fritz Krauskopf in Königsberg, she learned that photography was used as a propaganda tool and that the Reich encouraged soldiers to take photos as a way of strengthening the connection between the soldiers' homes and their lives at the front. Nearly every home had a portrait of a dashing infantryman or *Luftwaffe* pilot proudly displayed on the fireplace mantel or parlor table. Inge wondered if her job would be to catalog these images. She hoped not. She wanted to be the one who took the photos and developed them, not the one who organized and cataloged them. She hoped that she would be an assistant, helping to prepare portraits and develop negatives, and maybe become a photographer herself one day. Leni Riefenstahl was an actress who went on to become one of the most famous film directors in the Reich, renowned for her artistry with light and composition and motion. *If a woman can be one of Germany's greatest movie directors, Inge thought, surely I can learn to be a great photographer.*

She smiled when she thought back to the antics she and her best friend, who was also named Inge (she called her Ingeline), pulled at Krauskopf. The studio was where all the Wehrmacht officers came to have their formal military photos taken. Many of them were still quite young. Inge would sneak out the duplicates, then she and Ingeline entertained themselves by inventing stories about the more handsome ones. "This one is Herr Grönemeyer, a combat stenographer who is stationed on the dangerous Swiss frontier. He is betrothed to the banker's daughter, but is secretly in love with the girl who feeds the monkeys at the zoo. They passionately embrace in the monkey house, then he goes to his fiancé stinking worse than her dog." They collapsed in fits of laughter, every story outdoing the last one. In retrospect, she imagined that the two of them could have been severely punished if they were discovered, but she thought the fun they had together was worth the risk.

Inge took the tram across the city and arrived at the Photography Institute, the anxiety of a new adventure knotted in the pit of her stomach. Herr Gunter Alberts met her with a broad smile and an enthusiastic "Guten Morgen, Fräulein." His short dwarf-like frame matched the elfen twinkle in his eye. Inge felt instantly drawn to him, a refreshing change from the taciturn Frau Epler. He would be her boss and mentor, and she hoped that working for him would brighten her new life in Leipzig.

The institute was a cavernous building, three stories of endless formal rooms in which to stage portraits. The basement held the darkrooms. Walking downstairs, the acrid, metallic stench of developing chemicals assaulted her nose, but she was used to it. It felt familiar. It felt like home.

The Photography Institute was a fast-paced environment, but Inge soon grew accustomed to it. Her primary duty was to help stage portraits. She enjoyed the work. There was an air of propriety as she was given complete freedom to help clients find the most flattering poses. She loved to use her imagination to create back stories for the people in the photographs.

As much as she enjoyed the work, over time it became routine and monotonous. What at first seemed like an endless variety of creative solutions to posing portraits eventually became dull and boring. There were only so many ways to arrange a couple, a family, or a group of children. A year had passed since she arrived in Leipzig; it was now 1940 and she wasn't enjoying it as she had hoped she would. Frau Epler's house was suffocating, and the photography studio was tedious. This wasn't developing into the extraordinary life that Inge craved. It was beginning to feel like a roadblock.

Inge also began to realize that the world was not as she imagined. The reality of war was crawling forth, and it was casting a pall over the life of the city. Just last year Britain and France had declared war and, in response, the German army had invaded the Netherlands, Belgium, and France. Inge had never been particularly interested in politics, but she could no longer avoid it. She began to understand the difference between a political party, such as the Nazis, and the Wehrmacht, which was the unified military force. Her father had no love for the Nazis, but when recalled to duty he had no choice but to comply. His loyalty was to Germany. The Nazis were loyal to Adolf Hitler. The Nazis had done their best to make it seem as though the country and the party were one and that both were united and embodied in the person of Hitler. They had even replaced the national flag with the party flag, and made the party emblem, the swastika, an unavoidable part of daily life. Ordinary people greeted one another with the phrase *Heil Hitler,* a constant reminder of the role that the party now played in the life of the nation. Wehrmacht uniforms were emblazoned with Nazi swastikas, and Inge's father wore a Wehrmacht uniform, but he was no Nazi. The distinction hadn't meant much to her before, but it was becoming impossible not to think about it. In Königsberg she had moved in only a small group of people. Now, in Leipzig, she knew many more, from all parts of the Reich. And they told her stories about late-night visits from the Gestapo, and of people disappearing without explanation—particularly Jews. She remembered her Jewish girlfriends from school, Henriette and Hannah, who were absent one day and never returned. She assumed they had moved away and hadn't thought much about it, other than being hurt and slightly angry that they didn't bother to say goodbye. For the first time, Inge recognized that her experience of the war was less intense than that of many other people. Her only awareness was what she heard on the radio and saw in newspapers and the fact that she experienced shortages and had to deal with rationing of food. She had a job, she had friends, she had the freedom of the city. Others were fighting the war, mourning the deaths of their sons and fathers, or imprisoned because the party felt that they were a threat. Like Henriette and Hannah, who didn't say goodbye. Where were they now? And how could she have been so selfish?

These thoughts unsettled her, and she tried to calm them by focusing on her duties at the Institute. On Monday morning there was a portrait booking for a chemistry student who was applying for a fellowship and needed a photograph. Herr Alberts said, "Inge, this is an important young man. We must make a good impression on him. He comes from a prominent Leipzig family and could lead to more business." Inge prepared the Library Room as the ideal background for an academic setting. The young man arrived early and introduced himself merely as Henri. Inge thought to herself *he must think everyone knows who his family is.* When she got a better look, she was speechless. He was tall with slim hips, the features that had always stuck Inge as the ideal male, and he had an aristocratic air of privilege. She was totally taken by him.

Henri sauntered into the studio and stood before the bookshelf with a stance of superiority. Inge quietly adjusted the lighting and assisted Herr Alberts in highlighting his best features. Henri didn't seem to notice Inge's appreciative looks. He was too self-involved in finding the right angles for his portrait. He spoke to Herr Alberts of his plan to go to Vienna to further his chemistry studies and apply for a fellowship in Marburg afterward. He caught her eye once, during the portrait session, and held it for a moment before focusing again on the camera. His gaze betrayed something more than just a casual interest. Inge wondered if he was really as arrogant and pompous as he seemed to be or if he just affected that attitude when among strangers.

She didn't see Henri again for a few weeks. He was scheduled to come back to pick up his finished prints, and she was looking forward to the encounter. She had seen a glimpse of the human being beneath the stuffy façade and she wanted a chance to find out who he really was.

Then she saw it in the appointment book: On Thursday at five o'clock Henri would return to review his prints. Inge picked out a special outfit for the occasion. She didn't have an extensive wardrobe anymore because she couldn't afford much on her salary, but she knew how to put an outfit together and how to make the most of what she had. Her green blouse would accentuate her eyes, and her black skirt would highlight her figure. Any man with a pulse would be smitten. Henri wouldn't be able to take his eyes off of her.

When he arrived, as erect and distinguished as before, she saw to it that she was the one who would attend to him. They sat together in the small room, just a few feet apart, the bracing aroma of Henri's aftershave tickling her nostrils, only the two of them, alone. Inge bowed her head over the prints, then cast her eyes up to him and smiled. She selected three shots and arranged them before him. "These look distinguished and should help you get that fellowship," she said. "They show a serious, determined man who has important goals."

Henri slumped a little in his chair as a weak smile crept across his lips. "Thank you," he said. "I wish that were true." He told her that he was the youngest son of a prominent family of noble heritage. "My father has plans for me. The war has been difficult for us, and we have lost nearly everything. My father hopes that I will restore the family fortune and reclaim our honor." Henri showed her his hand. He wore a massive gold ring with his family crest. "It's an awful burden. Every day I'm stricken with the knowledge of what he expects of me. It's overwhelming. Every day I wish I could leave it all behind and escape. But I know that I can't."

Inge's instincts had been correct. Still, she was stunned by how easily and thoroughly his defenses had crumbled. He was frightened and insecure, determined to be the man that his family needed him to be, but entirely unsure of his ability to play that role. Their conversation grew comfortable, and Henri asked if she would join him at the café for a pastry. Inge joyfully accepted, with the giddy hopes of romance and a budding new relationship filling her head. Over coffee and pastries Henri said, "I'm moving to Vienna to attend the university, and then I've been accepted to the fellowship in Marburg. But, until then, I would love to get to know you better." Inge almost choked on her marzipan.

They spent Henri's last weeks in Leipzig going to parties and enjoying themselves. In June 1941, shortly before Henri was due to leave, they sat in his apartment and listened to Hitler's radio address about a surprise attack on the Soviet Union—Operation Barbarossa:

German people! At this moment, an attack unprecedented in the history of the world in its extent and size has begun. I have decided today to put the fate of Germany and the future of the German Reich and our people in the hands of our soldiers. May God help us in this battle.

Hearing Hitler's voice reminded Inge of her youth in Königsberg. She told Henri, "I remember that I was expected to attend the German League of Girls, Hitler's *Bund Deutscher Mädel*. We were told to dedicate ourselves to comradeship, service, and physical fitness for motherhood. The worst was that we had to wear these awful navy-blue skirts, white blouses, brown jackets, and put our hair in twin pigtails. It was awful. That all wasn't for me." Inge smiled at the thought that, of all things, it was the uniform that had annoyed her the most. "My friend Ingeline and I didn't want to belong to a group that told us what to do and what to think and especially what to wear. When we were supposed to attend the weekly meetings, we went to see American movies instead. I'm sure we could have gotten into trouble for this, but nobody ever knew. They never bothered to check." Henri laughed and shook his head at her rebellious spirit. Why hadn't he had had the courage to be so free?

Inge continued. "A few years later there was no way for me to avoid the obligation of compulsory work at *Arbeitsdienst*, the labor service. Everyone had to participate and it was taken much more seriously than the *Bund Deutscher Mädel*." Inge thought about her assignment. "This was real work and everyone was expected to do her part. They sent us to the site of an old mansion where we tended cows. I'm a city girl; I had never even met a cow. Can you imagine?" She remembered the morning her mother took her to the train station and waved goodbye. Inge was going to be gone for six months. She was apprehensive about leaving home for the unknown, but she thought it might be good practice for the future. Many other girls, equally young and unsure, filled the train. Inge wanted to make a good impression because she knew these were going to be her companions for the next half-year.

She laughed at she shared with Henri her first encounter with a cow. "I looked around at the meadows and farmyard. Everything was peaceful and quiet and I was focused on the wildflowers. I expected the aroma of fresh flowers but as I took in a deep breath all I smelled was rotten eggs. I couldn't place it. Then I heard the clanking of a bell and turned around. Behind me was a group of cows, just staring at me. I had never been up close to a cow and didn't know how to react."

Inge grew quiet and looked away. She thought about her home, her mother, and the memories of happy times. "Yes, I know that *Arbeitsdienst* was supposed to be serious labor and we were supposed to contribute to the *Vaterland*, but for me it turned out to be a lot of fun. I was with a wonderful group of girls and we had such a good time putting on play productions and laughing late into the night." Inge shyly confessed that sometimes she felt guilty about it. She knew that there were others who had a much harder time. Since then she had grown to know just how lucky she was.

Henri smiled. He was getting to know Inge better and realized what a kind heart she had. Her sense of freedom and adventure attracted him. Could he build a future with her? He would soon leave for Vienna. What could he give her as a promise for the future? He thought of his ring with the family crest. He wanted to give her a symbol of his connection to his family and planned to give her a gold ring with a round blue surface that would hold his family crest when she accepted his hand in marriage.

The night before Henri's departure he arrived on Frau Epler's doorstep and said to Inge, "I've planned a wonderful evening for us. I know how much you love jazz and dancing. For my last night here, we are going out on the town." Inge felt a mixture of joy and sadness, but for this night she would let the joy prevail.

Henri took her by the hand and they walked through the streets of Leipzig to a nightclub that had a swing band. They found their way through the dim, smoky light and maneuvered around the small round tables until they found one of their own. Inge was enchanted by the music and tapped her foot to the beat. She loved to dance, and the music was captivating.

They ordered drinks; Inge's was a French Pernod which was her favorite anise drink. It made her feel sophisticated and it quickly went to her head. Henri enjoyed seeing Inge have such a good time and he felt a sadness at leaving her in Leipzig while he finished his studies in Vienna. He reached for her hand. "Inge, you know I'll be gone for a year. After I finish in Vienna I'll go to Marburg. Leave Leipzig and wait for me there." His heart beat faster. "As a symbol of my devotion and promise I give you this gold ring that, if you agree to marry me, will one day hold my family crest."

This was certainly more than Inge expected from their night on the town. Of course she would accept his ring. She was delighted. She was ready to move forward in her life and starting an adventure with Henri was a wonderful development. Besides, Marburg seemed like a nice city in the middle of Germany. She no longer felt safe in Leipzig because of the increasing attacks by British and American bombers. The most severe one occurred on December fourth and claimed almost two thousand lives.

Inge remembered her first air raid and how frightened she had been. She and her friend Helga, from the institute, had gone to the movies. Halfway through the show they heard someone shout that they heard the air raid warning. Inge turned to Helga and saw the terror in her eyes. The house lights came on and everyone streamed toward the exit. "What are we going to do?" asked Helga in a voice quaking with fear. Inge didn't know, but she grabbed Helga's hand and pulled her outside into the street. The shrill sirens pierced their eardrums. They looked into the sky and saw the powerful searchlights spotting the bombers high above them. Booming antiaircraft fire shook the pavement and resonated in their skulls. People fled in every direction, parents calling for children, young couples fleeing hand-in-hand, a bewildered old man on crutches helped by a Wehrmacht soldier, a loose dog scurrying and barking among the crowd. Among them, Inge and Helga felt their feet planted in the ground, transfixed by the chaos. Then a boom that sucked the very air from their lungs. A glowing inferno blossomed over the rooftops, turning the night sky to a sickening orange. Helga, tears tracking down her face, shouted at Inge, but she could hear only a deafening ring that pushed away every other sound. She shook her head and forced herself to think. *We have to move.* They ran to a nearby house shelter. At first the man who lived there wouldn't let them in, but his wife took pity and allowed them to enter. Doors banged, windows cracked, and household objects fell all around. Inge's teeth chattered with nervous adrenaline. She imagined her mother receiving the news of her death, an air raid casualty far away from home in Leipzig.

When the bombing stopped, and the all-clear sounded, Inge looked at her watch. Twenty minutes had passed. It had seemed like hours.

Inge and Helga thanked the house owners for allowing them to shelter, then they stepped outside into a different world. There sky was aglow with the flames of allied bombs, and fire brigades crisscrossed the streets, doing their best to keep the infernos from spreading. Inge said "I never want to be that scared again," but the air raids continued and soon they were a part of their daily lives.

As much as she didn't want to think about it, and as much as she tried to get along as if everything were normal, Inge was shocked and frightened. Large parts of the city center were destroyed. How many people had lost their lives? How many families no longer had places to call home? She didn't want to stay alone in Leipzig. A move to a different area might be a good choice.

Everything happened quickly, and a month later she found herself in Marburg. She was thrilled to say farewell to Frau Epler, and once again Inge's mother was able to pave the path for her from a distance. Through connections with old acquaintances who had left Königsberg, Inge met Grete and Louisa who lived in a farmhouse on the outskirts of the city. They were looking for a third roommate, and Inge was happy to oblige. She moved in.

The year waiting for Henri's return moved slowly, but Inge didn't allow herself to get bored. She liked Grete and Louisa and they spent long evenings in their house listening to Benny Goodman records. Louisa was shy and felt uncomfortable dancing, but Inge would say "Come on Louisa, I'll show you how to move your feet to the beat of the music." Grete, on the other hand, was a natural and they spent their evenings coaching Louisa around their big living room.

Inge was lucky enough to be able to transfer her position to the Marburg Institute of Photography where her job was to take photographs of student-produced artworks. She enjoyed her work, but was beginning to get impatient. Henri couldn't get there fast enough to suit her. She was anxious for June and their much anticipated reunion.

Henri was due to arrive in Marburg on June seventeenth. Inge was excited. She had waited long enough. As the date came closer, she felt both apprehension and exhilaration. Once she was reunited with Henri she knew that her life would be back on track. She kept a calendar by her bedside and, like a prisoner, she would X out each day as his arrival approached. She created a mental tally of what could go wrong—*Does he still love me? Did he find someone* else? Is he ready to make good on his promise of a future together?* She kept telling herself that nothing had changed between them. His letters continued to be love-filled, and he spoke about his desire to be by her side once again. Inge wished that time would hurry up so that her fears and questions would be settled.

June seventeenth finally arrived. Inge spent the night before preparing for the day. She wanted Henri to be impressed with her and elated at their reunion. As she left the farmhouse to go to the train station, she saw two love birds on the porch. An omen of the future! The fluttery feeling in her stomach grew as she approached the station. She wanted everything to be magical, but still felt some apprehension that her expectations would be shattered.

Henri stood on the platform, the tall, thin man she had grown fond of and was so looking forward to seeing again. She had been ready to begin a life together with him, but when she saw him she was taken aback by her reaction. *She felt nothing.* She had expected to be overcome with joy at the sight of him. She wanted to be overcome with joy. Instead, while she was pleased to see him, she wasn't pleased in the way she had expected to be. Not pleased enough. She said to herself, *Ignore this feeling. It means nothing. You haven't seen him for a year; you are not used to seeing him. Soon the old feelings will return.* Yet, given what was happening in her own head, she couldn't help but wonder what Henri felt.

They embraced when he stepped from the platform. He said he was so glad to see her and couldn't wait to return to their happy times together. At that moment, Inge made the decision to bury her feelings. After all, this was the man she would likely marry, and she wanted to be happy with him.

He said, "As soon as I get settled in, I want you to come and meet my parents. I've told them all about you and they're anxious to get to know you." Inge was unsettled by the prospect of meeting his parents. She knew they were a socially prominent, affluent family of noble decent. How would they feel about her as the bride of their shining star, Henri?

She felt intimidated and she hated that feeling. She wanted to make a good impression. When she arrived at Henri's home, a charming three-story building, Henri opened the door and welcomed her in with a hug. As he escorted her through the entrance hall he whispered, "Don't worry, they're not as bad as they seem. They'll love you as much as I do." Inge smiled and walked into the lavish living room. Seated on the sofa was a queenly woman and a regal looking man. They were imposing, but they were also polite and gracious and they greeted her warmly. They had many questions about her family and her childhood in Königsberg. Why were they so curious about her background, especially her decision to leave Königsberg to work at the Photography Institute? Inge kept looking over at Henri and expecting him to intervene. She asked herself, *Why is he allowing this inquisition?* But he never said a thing; he only averted his eyes and looked away.

In the following weeks Inge and Henri continued to have a good time and spent most evenings together, but Inge felt that things weren't quite the same as they were before. Something was missing between them. She couldn't put words to it, but something had shifted. She couldn't sort her feelings. They didn't talk about it and they both pretended everything was fine, but she could tell that Henri felt differently too. She had expected him to ask her to marry him and she wasn't sure what she would say if he did. She was glad that he hadn't.

One night in late August, Henri was scheduled to pick her up for dinner. Inge prepared for the evening as she always did, carefully selecting her outfit and fixing her hair and makeup. Going out with Henri had become routine. She looked forward to it, but not with the same excitement as before. When he arrived she could tell he had something on his mind. She held her breath in anticipation.

Henri said, "Inge, let's sit down. We have to talk." Whatever he had to talk about, it was obviously important. "We've had a lot of fun together and I've grown so fond of you. But… I don't believe we have a promising future together. I had a long talk with my parents. They think you're a special woman, but they're worried that you might be too independent." Inge was silent. She could handle him becoming bored with her, or feeling that they just weren't right for each other, but *too independent?* She thought that this was exactly what he loved most about her. Maybe it was, but if he allowed his feelings to be so easily swept aside by his parents' opinion, then he certainly wasn't who she had hoped he could be. And she knew that he wasn't for her.

Inge found her words but hid her pain. "Henri, you've always known that I want to live an extraordinary life. I thought you and I might find this together. It seems I was wrong." Inge stood up, kissed his cheek, and escorted him to the door.

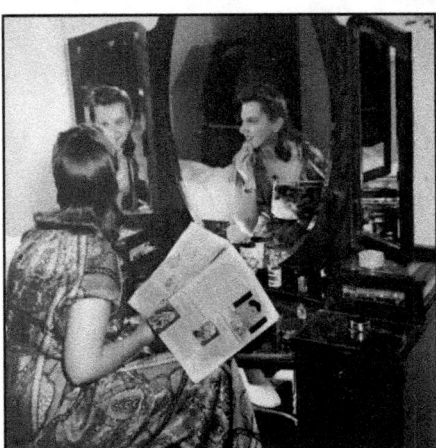

Inge in her Königsberg bedroom looking at magazines and dreaming of an exceptional life.

Inge and Henri

Henri posing for photos at the studio in Liepzig.

The Other Side of Ordinary

Inge and the other girls at the obligation of compulsory work at Arbeitsdienst, *the labor service.*

2

Marburg
December 1944

INGE WAS RESTLESS. WINTER was looming, and the air outside was crisp. She was tired of war. Earlier that year she heard stories of what was being called D-Day, when the Allies landed in Normandy. In the East, the Soviet army edged ever closer. Like the rest of the German people, Inge could see the writing on the wall: The war was lost. Everyone carried on as best they could, but a pall of morbid suspense had fallen across their lives, as if the ending had been written but someone pulled out the pages in between.

This evening she was waiting for Helmuth who was to take her to dinner. She needed a distraction from the heartbreak and boredom she felt after her break-up with Henri. Although she and Helmuth were only friends, she still took special care with her appearance. After all, she never knew who else she might meet. Elegance continued to be her hallmark; she picked a black flowing skirt with a gray sweater that accentuated her figure.

When Helmuth arrived at the apartment, he said, "Inge, I promised to take you to dinner, but first I have to stop by my friend's house and drop off the book I borrowed."

Inge was hungry and was looking forward to dinner. Because of the long years of war, food was becoming sparse and unpredictable. Eating out was such a treat. She hoped the errand wouldn't take long.

Inge was surprised to find herself at a three-story building with a white iron gate in front and a brick pathway to the door. It looked like an old college or an art gallery, not a private home. As they walked up the path, Inge felt a conspicuous, penetrating glare. She glanced up. A man watched intensely from the second-floor window, focused solely upon her. Helmuth sensed her unease. "Don't worry about that man. That's my friend's father; he's an odd, mysterious character. I understand he has quite an interesting background, but he never talks much about him."

Helmuth rang the bell. They waited. No response. Helmuth rang again. The door creaked open. Before them stood a man who looked like he had just taken a three-hour nap. His wrinkled clothes hung loosely on his frame, his feet were bare, and his thin, uncombed hair poked out in every direction. He rubbed his eyes and shook the fog from his head, then broke into a big, friendly smile, his eyes crinkling at the corners. "Helmuth!" he said, throwing his arms wide for an embrace. "Please, come inside. I am so sorry for the way I look." He tipped an imaginary hat to Inge. "I must be making a terrible impression, but I worked all night at the clinic."

Helmuth said, "Inge, I would like you to meet my good friend, Cuauhtémoc Krumm-Heller. We call him *Moc*. He just graduated from medical school and is working so hard at the Marburg Hospital that he naps all day when he's at home."

Inge giggled inwardly. *Cuauhtémoc, what a curious name. I'm glad he has a short nickname because I would never remember that.* She asked, "Cuauhtémoc? Where does that name come from?"

Moc smiled. He had been answering this question for years. "Cuauhtémoc was the last Aztec emperor of Mexico. My father lived there for many years and named me in honor of the culture. It isn't an easy name to carry."

The moment Helmuth handed Moc the book he had borrowed there was the ear-splitting shriek of an air-raid alarm. By now they were accustomed to the frequent air raids because the Allies had been bombing German cities since March 1943. Although still worrisome, they were no longer cause for panic. They were almost routine. Besides, Marburg had suffered little damage from bombings because it had been designated a *hospital city* and many of its buildings doubled as wards. However, Inge and Helmuth immediately realized that they couldn't leave. Inge thought back to the terror of her first air-raid in Leipzig, of the panic and fear that had gripped her and the people of the city. Now air raids were so common that this one only meant a change of dinner plans. They were destined to spend the evening with Moc.

Their host waved to an extravagant sofa and invited them to make themselves comfortable. They sank into the thick cushions, engulfed as if in a cocoon. Despite being used to the air raids, a sense of anxiety still hung in the room. They had endured countless raids without incident, but there was always a chance that tonight could be different. Moc did his best to make them feel at ease. He hurried to the kitchen to prepare coffee and brought out some leftover cookies from the night before.

The trio passed the time chatting. Inge was enthralled by Moc's stories of his family and their adventures. He said, "I've lived my entire life hearing stories about Mexico." He went on to weave the story of his father's involvement in the Mexican revolution and becoming a German spy. When his father gained Mexican citizenship, he returned to Germany as the Mexican military attaché. This explained why Moc held Mexican citizenship and did not have to enlist in the German army. Moc went on to say, "I'm fascinated by Mexico. My father left me and my older sister, Guadalupe, behind and took Parsivald, my younger brother, on all the Mexican adventures. I've always felt left out, and I plan to move there someday to make my fortune."

Inge told Moc about how she had left Königsberg, and her separation from her parents. Moc sensed Inge's sadness and heartache. To distract her and to lighten the mood, he brought out a deck of cards.

He fanned the cards before Inge and Helmuth, dealt four jacks face-up in four separate piles, and spun a tale.

"The jacks were having a party, and they invited their friends, the kings." He placed a king on each of the jacks. "They got a little bored, so they invited the queens to liven up the party." He placed a queen on each of the piles. "Now the party was getting a little rowdy, so the police," Moc placed an ace on each pile, "came and took them all to jail. Along the way, the police cars got into an accident." He shuffled the cards and dealt them one out one at a time. To Inge and Helmuth's surprise and delight, the aces, kings, queens, and jacks were still in their separate piles together. "Even though they were separated in the accident, when they arrived at the station they were all together."

As interesting as the card trick was, it was Moc's face that held Inge's attention. His eyes sparkled with enthusiasm as he built the suspense. When he glanced away from the cards and caught her eye with a smile, she wondered if his sleight of hand was done for her benefit. *Is he trying to impress me?* she wondered. *Well, it's working.*

After her crumbling involvement with Henri, Inge was reluctant to get pulled into another relationship. She was going to be careful, but still, she felt a slight echoing in her heart. Maybe there was room to start again.

Helmuth sat back and watched the two of them. The spark between them was obvious. He loved both his friends, but he hadn't planned on being a matchmaker. He felt destiny had brought them together this night and his job was to get out of the way and allow Providence to prevail.

The *all-clear* bell sounded late that night. They were

all glad to have permission to resume their normal activities, but Inge felt a twinge of sadness that the evening was over. When she and Helmuth left the apartment, she turned to him and said, "Hmm, that Moc fellow is interesting."

Inge was intrigued by Moc, but her life at the photography studio was busy enough to make socializing difficult. She continued to catalog the photos and build the archives. She didn't think about him again until late December when Helmuth told her Moc was hosting a huge New Year's Eve party. He asked, "Do you want to go? You already know him, and it should be fun."

Inge was always ready for a party, and there were so few of them now. And Moc would be there. She dug through her wardrobe finding just the right outfit, settling on a black straight skirt with fringes at the bottom. She looked like a festive 1920s flapper, just the right tone for New Year's Eve. Inge surprised herself by how much she hoped Moc would notice her and appreciate the way she looked.

When she and Helmuth arrived Moc saw her immediately. A shy smile crossed his face. He was obviously pleased to see her. She returned his smile and felt her cheeks flush. The house was filled with her friends and acquaintances; she and Moc had so many friends in common, how had they gone so long without meeting? She assessed the other women in attendance and compared herself to them. Even when dressed in their best party gowns they couldn't compete with Inge. She felt the men's eyes upon her, saw how they nervously fumbled their speech when they spoke to her, and sensed the jealousy of their companions. She was electrifying and she knew it.

Inge made small talk with the other guests, but her attention always drifted back to Moc. She checked him from the corner of her eye every few minutes, keeping tabs on where he was and to whom he was speaking. Once, she captured his gaze from across the room and gave him a flirtatious smile and a wink, putting him slightly off balance. He almost seemed to be keeping his distance from her, as if he and Inge were on opposite sides of a wheel as they rotated among the crowd. But when Moc took her by the arm and led her to a secluded divan in the corner of the room she realized that he had been saying hello to everyone else so that he could spend more time with her. They spent the hours in deep conversation, and he revealed things about himself that Inge suspected he didn't share with many others.

Moc opened the gate to his story with a tight jaw and a hint of sadness. He leaned forward and said, "My father traveled throughout Latin America and studied the anthropology of Inca tribes in the Andes. He learned about the Inca god Huirucocha and he adopted it as his spiritual name. Still today there are many followers of my father throughout Latin America who call him Huirucocha."

Inge could only imagine Moc's lonely childhood, being left behind in Berlin while his younger brother got to travel with his parents.

Moc continued, "My father is a spiritualist and mystic. He worked as a traveling therapist in the rainforests of Bolivia. He was particularly interested in osmology, the study of odors, their production, and their effect. He claims he can identify different Indian tribes by the smell of their sweat. He was also an occultist who was deeply involved with the O.T.O and the Rosicrucian Order." Inge sensed by the tension in his voice and his rigid posture that Moc's relationship with his father wasn't a good one.

Inge was captivated by Moc, and she hoped he was with her as well. She wanted the evening to revolve only around the two of them, but the party intruded. Everyone knew this was a heavy holiday. The New Year was the brink of a new reality for Germany, and despite the forced gaiety, everyone felt the burden of what was to come.

By midnight, the weight of the mood started to pass. It was 1945. The guests struggled to enjoy themselves and pretend they weren't preoccupied with the onrushing armies that would soon change all of their lives. Inge knew that this would be a memorable and historic year—and a dangerous one—for her and for all of Germany.

The next morning, Inge listened with Luisa and Gretel to the radio reports of the Luftwaffe's Operation Bodenplatte, aimed at attacking Allied airfields in France—Allied airfields that should have been in Britain. This seemed like a last, desperate effort, and it was clear that time was running out. How much longer would it be before their world collapsed around them? Inge was nervous and scared.

When she was a child, she indulged her nerves by biting her fingernails. She stopped when a handsome young man said to her, "Inge, I can't believe you have such a disgusting habit." She never bit them again. But, at this moment, she really needed to bite her nails.

Although Inge expected life to change rapidly, she was surprised to find that everything continued as before. With snow still on the ground, there was an atmosphere of normalcy, but also an underlying sense of apprehension. In Marburg, a spirit of resignation prevailed as surrender loomed. Against orders to the contrary, the city was prepared to place itself at the mercy of the invading armies without resistance.

On the morning of March 28th a broadcast warned that American forces were approaching Marburg from Giessen. Inge didn't know what to expect. She had always admired American movies and music, yet she couldn't imagine what American soldiers would be like. Would they be haughty and domineering? Would they raid their homes, burn their towns, and press Inge and her friends into service? She thought about the horrors that the Red Army had perpetrated in the East. The Americans couldn't be that bad. *Could they?* That day she stayed home from work and huddled in the farmhouse with Louisa and Grete, nervously pacing the floors, expecting the worst but hoping for the best. They played Benny Goodman records to set the mood for the American occupation, and maybe to let the troops know that there were friends inside. Because the farmhouse was on the road to Giessen, they realized that the invading army would march right past their home.

Louisa and Grete sat on the front porch and called Inge to come and join them. Louisa said, "Look, I see green uniforms in the distance."

Grete added, "They're carrying rifles and wearing helmets." It was an image that Inge knew would forever be etched in her memory. Her heartbeat accelerated and her senses tingled. When they came closer, she was stunned to see ordinary looking young men, most of them chewing gum and needing a shave. It wasn't an invading horde. Her pulse slowed, her breathing returned to normal, and a wave of relief washed over her. She sensed that she had nothing to fear from these men. Some of them even waved as they marched past.

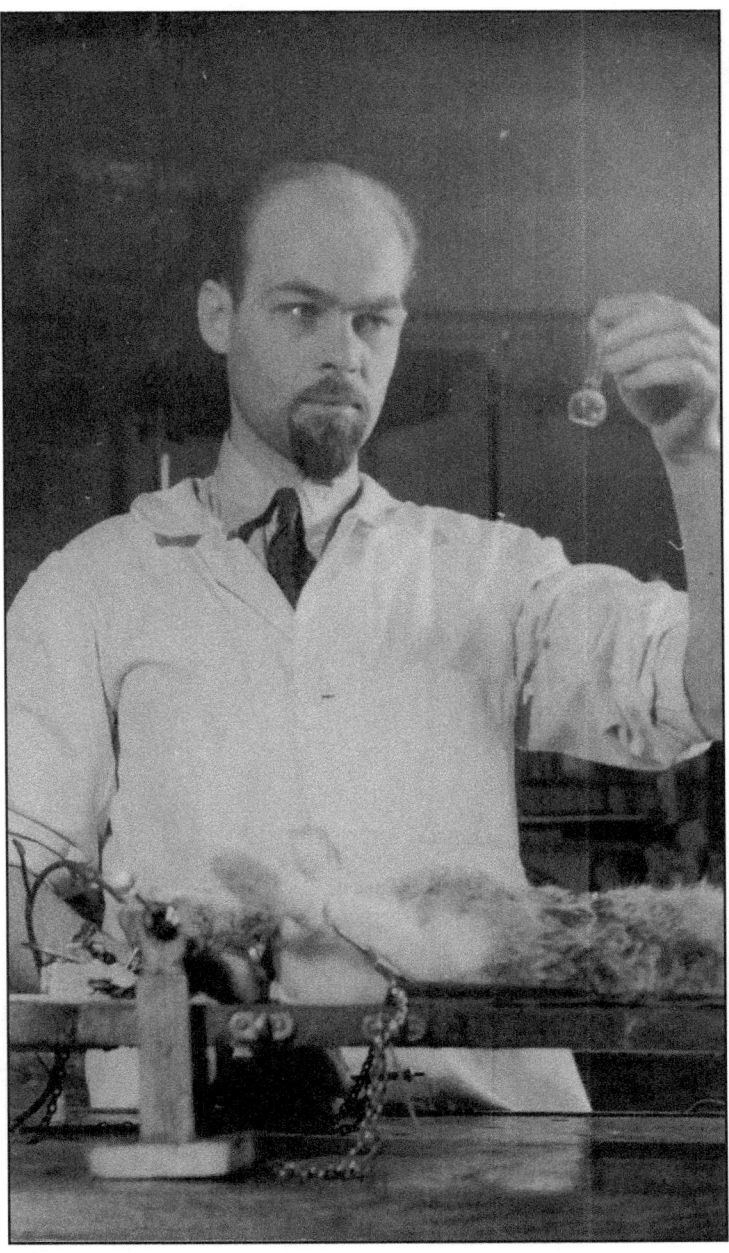

Moc in the lab.

Inge in Marburg.

3

Marburg
May 1945

AFTER SO MANY MONTHS of cold weather and snow, Inge sought a renewed sense of optimism. On impulse, she decided to walk downtown to the café to buy herself a pastry. A handsome young man strolled towards her. There was something familiar about him. What was it? Maybe it was his gait. She searched her memories, but she couldn't place him. Then she saw his thinning hair and his intense blue eyes: It was Moc.

He smiled when he saw her and kissed her hand. They hadn't seen each other since the New Year's Eve party, both preoccupied with the rapidly changing situation around them and the hardships of life under occupation.

Moc reached into his pocket and, to Inge's amazement, produced an American Lucky Strike cigarette. To Inge, it may as well have been the Hope Diamond. She placed it between her lips and Moc lit it for her. She took a grateful drag of the scarce tobacco and felt the familiar rush of nicotine hit her brain. Moc said, "I've been lucky. I have a placement with the Americans. They needed a driver to help them know the city. Since I'm not a German citizen, they felt I was a good choice. My boss is Mr. Teal; he's very generous." He waved the pack of Lucky Strikes before her eyes as evidence.

"I've been thinking about you, Inge. I'm sorry we lost touch after the party. I'd like to see you again."

Inge smiled shyly. "I would like that too."

They walked together and ended up at the entrance of the park. It was a lovely spring day, and they strolled along the meandering, treelined paths, surrounded by the lawns and the budding trees. Moc took Inge's hand. They didn't say much. The joy of their reunion required no expression beyond the warm clasp of their hands. They were together and that was enough.

Inge sat on a park bench, pulling Moc down beside her. She wanted to enjoy this moment. It felt so strange to be in such an oasis after all that had happened in Marburg. It was easy to forget the war and the foreboding about what was to come. Although life had settled into a comfortable routine during the occupation, there was still uncertainty. She heard the birds chirp and the squirrels chatter as they leaped from tree to tree. How wonderfully oblivious they all were, she thought. She was pleased to see that even in the turmoil of the American occupation, and the ambiguity about what was to come, the people still cared for the city's sanctuary spots.

Others strolled by, many looking like lovers beginning new lives amid the ruins. She wanted to feel safe, like she imagined they felt having loved ones in their lives. She felt numb. Was it loneliness? Inge watched the couples and wondered, *Could this be where Moc and I are heading with this relationship? I hardly know him. But it would be nice to care for someone again and to feel safe.*

Even though Inge wasn't sure about where her relationship with Moc might lead, she felt confident and content sitting next to him. They had a connection, and both felt safe sharing their inner thoughts. Moc looked at Inge and opened his heart to her.

"This is a difficult time for me. My mother had been seriously ill. She had stomach cancer." He went on to tell the story of his mother lying in bed when his father heard a knock on the door. "When he answered the door, a group of Nazi officers pushed through like locusts. They demanded to see my father's precious library. He treasured his library and was devastated if he lost even one volume. They seized any books by Jewish authors, many of which my father had rescued from a book burning. Then they told him to consider himself lucky that they were only confiscating his books and not arresting him." Moc's face was grim. "My father was devastated by the loss of his books, but that was only the beginning. We celebrated my mother's forty-ninth birthday on April 24th, and she died three days later." His eyes filled with tears, just as Inge felt her own tears gather and trickle down her cheeks. She was surprised by her reaction to his pain. The numbness she had felt was gone, replaced by a churning stomach and a heaviness in her chest.

Moc's demeanor changed as his shoulders grew slack.

"My father gave me my mother's favorite ring as a remembrance. It's a ring that he designed for her, and it holds a mystery. On the front is the symbol for Virgo, his astrological sign, and inside there are symbols of alchemy and magical signs of celestial hierarchies designed to provide protection. It's special to me and will always remind me of her."

Moc's loss reminded Inge of her own. She told him about losing contact with her parents. The news about the evacuation of East Prussia was terrifying. She remembered the radio reports about the Red Army's offensive in early 1945. Once they were in Germany proper, the Soviet troops lost whatever restraint they had and launched a full-scale program of revenge. They destroyed villages, raped and killed women, and pillaged entire towns like a swarming medieval horde. The German government initiated a whirlwind evacuation of Königsberg in the face of the assault, but the situation quickly deteriorated into panic and chaos. Civilians poured in from the countryside, and millions of people, many of them children, the old, and the infirm, overwhelming the few means of transport that were still available. Some fled by foot and froze to death in the bitter cold, others chose routes that sent them directly into the maw of the Soviet war machine, and thousands boarded ocean transports only to be sent to the bottom of the Baltic Sea by lurking Soviet submarines. Tens of thousands were believed to have died, but the truth was that, in the lingering fog of war, no one knew the number. The only thing that Inge knew was that she hadn't heard from her mother. Had she stayed in Königsberg? Had she been able to leave? Inge couldn't bear to think about it.

Sharing their mutual tragedies drew Inge and Moc together. They met often, sharing afternoons in the park, consoling one another and sharing any hopeful news. One evening Moc invited her to come to a café to meet his boss, Mr. Teal. He was the first American that she met face to face and he was a little intimidating. He was tall and muscular, with wavy dark hair, just the image Inge had of an American movie star. She sat in admiring silence, surprised that he spoke such perfect German with no accent. He happily ate a slice of bienenstich, a pastry covered in almonds and honey with a creamy whipped filling. It was one of her favorite desserts. He offered one to Inge and she took a bite. In her state of awe she could barely taste it.

Mr. Teal told them and that his military unit was being reassigned. He spoke in a whisper, saying, "We have a great deal of leftover canned food. We can't take it with us, but I don't want it to go to waste. I'm not supposed to do this. Americans are here to liberate you, not to give you food, but I want to leave you the food anyway. Maybe you can hide it somewhere and use it."

Moc started thinking. "I can't keep it at my house. It's in the middle of town and would attract too much attention. But Inge lives on a farm outside of town. We could store it there." He turned to Inge. "What do you think?"

The next evening an army truck pulled up by Inge's

back door, and American soldiers unloaded boxes and boxes of canned food. Inge had never seen so much food in one place. She read the labels. There were Campbell's soups, something called *Spam* that looked like ham, tuna fish, peaches, tomato sauce, and many other things, some of which she recognized, and some of which were complete mysteries.

Moc and Inge agreed that he would come to her home every night and she would cook for him. He was astonished by her culinary skills. Inge found this quite comical because she wasn't much of a cook at all. Her talents lay in photography and fashion, not food. All she had to do was open the cans, dump them out, and heat it up. Inge laughed inwardly every time he complimented her.

Inge looked forward to seeing him arrive in the evenings. She was growing fond of him and she enjoyed his nightly dinner visits. One mid-May evening, Moc came at his usual time with a beautiful bouquet of white lilacs. He stood in front of her and said, "Inge, will you marry me? We have such a good time together, and I want you to come to Mexico with me. I can't imagine spending my life with anyone but you."

Inge's mind began to whirl. There was nothing keeping her in Germany. The country was in a shambles. She had lost her parents. Although she liked her job at the Photography Institute, it held no future. A new adventure beckoned. She had only known Moc for a short time, but she thought she might be in love with him. *Was she?* She could imagine their future together. He accepted her independence and didn't try to mold her into something she wasn't. That, alone, separated him from nearly every other man she knew. And her independent spirit was non-negotiable. "Yes," she said. "I will marry you."

The American occupation government was imposing rules and regulations. The rumor in town was that they would soon forbid marriages. Inge and Moc felt the pressure to have the wedding soon before the ordinance was enacted. One detail that hadn't occurred to them was that Inge would have to renounce her German citizenship to marry Moc since he was a Mexican citizen. Even though Hitler was gone, many of his rules remained. German women could not marry foreigners. What should she do? She thought of her parents and what they would say about their daughter not being a German. By renouncing her citizenship, Inge would become stateless, which meant she would have no country to call home, or any of the legal benefits and protections that come with citizenship. But Moc himself would be her new home, and she was ready for the next phase of her life, her extraordinary life, whatever it may bring.

Moc and Inge weren't the only ones in a hurry to marry before the American regulation was enacted. Louisa and Grete were going to marry, too. Grete had her mother's wedding dress, white satin with a lace collar, and the three girls decided they would share it, each one wearing it in turn. Inge wore it first.

On the morning of the wedding, as she stepped into

the dress, she appraised herself in the mirror. She saw her entire body, but she focused on one fault: on the right side of her stomach was an eight-inch ragged scar that traversed her belly. It made her feel deformed, but she could only slyly smile about the story behind it.

One morning, years ago, Inge woke up with a feeling of dread in her stomach. She had a math test that day, but hadn't adequately prepared for the exam. She lay in bed staring at the ceiling and plotting how to escape her fate. The slight discomfort she felt could be harnessed into a reason to stay home from school. She called out to her mother, feigning severe pain, and of course Inge's mother told her she must stay home. She smiled and burrowed down into the warm covers. When she awakened midmorning, she went downstairs and was thrilled to find her favorite meal waiting for her—Köngsberg Klöße. Inge ate it with relish but didn't want to reveal that she wasn't sick, so in spite of her obvious appetite she continued complaining about the pain in her belly.

Inge's mother was a cautious woman. She decided that since the stomach ache persisted, they needed to go to the hospital. Now Inge was trapped. She didn't want to get caught in the fib and let on that she had no pain, but she also didn't want to go to the doctor. She decided to go along, figuring that the doctor would find nothing wrong and send her back home.

In the hospital waiting room they were assaulted by the sharp aroma of antiseptic. They looked around at the sick people scattered about. Inge saw a mother with a crying baby, and an old man grimacing in pain. She instantly regretted her deception, but at this point she was too far gone to retreat.

Their name was called and they were ushered into the office of a brand-new handsome intern. Inge and her mother were told that she would be his first patient. Inge didn't know how to feel about this. It could be a good thing or not. He examined Inge's belly and confidently declared that she had appendicitis. Inge was appalled. Of course she didn't have appendicitis, but she couldn't give herself away. Her mother immediately arranged for the surgery and things spun further out of control.

Nausea descended. The Köngsberg Klöße wasn't a good choice for a pre-operative meal. She vomited, making a terrible mess, and then the incision in her belly brought excruciating pain. She was sure she was being punished for her deceit and would be cursed with an ugly scar made by a novice intern. She believed that he, too, now must realize that she didn't have appendicitis, but he couldn't reveal his incompetence to her or to his superiors. They were joined by their mutual secret. Next time she would be sure to study for the test.

This wasn't one of Inge's proudest moments, but now she could look back at it and laugh. She would share the story with Moc when he saw her scar. She blushed at the thought of him seeing her bare flesh.

But for now, she was focused on the wedding. They

didn't have money to buy rings. Moc, however, owned a small Colombian gold coin that his father had brought back from his travels in South America. He knew an honest jeweler who would give them a fair deal. He cut the coin in half and accepted one piece as payment for two brass rings. They kept the other half as a symbol of their future.

Moc reluctantly told Inge that his father disapproved of their marriage. He said, "Why do you marry her? She has nothing. When you go to Mexico, I know so many people who could find you a better wife." When Inge heard this, she remembered how hurt she was when Henri surrendered to his parents' objections and broke their engagement. She knew how difficult it must be for him to defy his father's wishes, and yet he had, and he had done it for her. She was glad that Moc had more of a backbone than Henri and didn't succumb to the pressure.

Inge felt the wedding would be lovely. Moc was friends with the mayor and he performed a civil ceremony in his office. The couple stood side by side, and Inge felt small in the grand book-lined office. She looked around and tried to etch into her memory the feel of the room and the magnitude of what they were about to do. She would promise to share her life with a man whom she had only known for a few months, but he shared her goals of an extraordinary life and was prepared to take her with him as they crafted their future together. If only there had been a photographer to capture the memory. Sadly, the Americans had taken all the cameras.

When the ceremony was over, Moc and Inge went to the small chapel to say their vows. This was a private moment and they didn't want anyone else to be there but the pastor. This time they faced each other, each looking into the other's eyes, and promised a life partnership. The tiny chapel had stained glass windows and wooden pews. She wished that her mother and father were there in the front seat and could share this special occasion with her. She missed them terribly but never as much as at this particular moment. By marrying Moc, she agreed to move forward and leave Germany behind. Her tears were of joy and sadness and they marked the beginning of a new life.

After the private ceremony, they shared their joy with friends at a small reception in Moc's backyard, as festive and extravagant as the postwar circumstances would allow. They had nothing to offer their guests the week before, but a case of wine had arrived for Moc's father. Moc appropriated it and traded it for flour, sugar, butter, and real coffee. His father would never miss the wine. Inge and Moc joked that it was his wedding gift. The housekeeper, who loved Moc, baked special cakes for the reception.

As the gathering was winding down an otherworldy figure in a white robe and hood appeared around the corner. Inge didn't know who it was and this frightened her. Even though the war was over, the times were still precarious, and surprise guests could be dangerous. She found Moc and interrupted his conversation. "What's happening?" she asked. Moc turned and his smile disappeared. He squeezed her arm. She glanced up in time to see him wipe the moisture from beneath his eyes before the tears could fall. "Don't worry," he said. She could hear the tightness in his throat. "It's my father. He's wearing his Rosicrucian regalia. It means he has accepted our marriage."

Inge searched her memory but came up empty. "What's a Rosicrucian?"

"He's part of the Rosicrucian community, a group of mystics who study and practice the metaphysical laws that govern the universe. They try to rediscover ancient knowledge, like alchemy and such. It's very important to him." And Inge could see how important his father's acceptance was to Moc.

Moc's father seemed to float rather than walk, and the chatter faded to silence as he moved across the room. He took center stage, commanding the crowd's attention, and spoke in a voice that oozed authority.

"I want to give you the metaphysical view and tell you about the alchemy of marriage. We understand how everything manifesting to us throughout the material world is the result of the sympathetic uniting or bonding of the negative and positive, the like and the unlike, the male and the female elements. In fact, the mystic realizes that it is only through the coming together and the uniting into one harmonious unit of two separate, but sympathetic and dissimilar, elements that we have manifestations of life, of form, or existence in any sense. Therefore, if we view marriage as the coming together by a natural alchemical law or principle of two separated but sympathetic complementary parts of a predetermined unit, we can understand that marriage under such conditions or of such a nature is an ideal state, and, in fact, the only state in which the two beings will find that phase or that degree of perfect manifestation and existence decreed by God and nature for them."

The guests stood in stunned and astonished silence. It seemed that Moc's father was providing a lecture on metaphysics to scholars rather than participating in the spirit of the occasion. Everyone understood that his words were deeply philosophical and way beyond the joyous atmosphere of the event, but they were polite and courteous and paid close attention to his words.

Inge and Moc tolerated the shift in mood since the evening was coming to a close anyway. They knew that this would likely be the last time they would be together with all of their friends because this occasion marked a turning point in Moc and Inge's life as they began their transition to living in a new world on a new continent.

Moc's mother

Moc and his father

Moc's father in Rosicrucian ceremonial dress

Moc

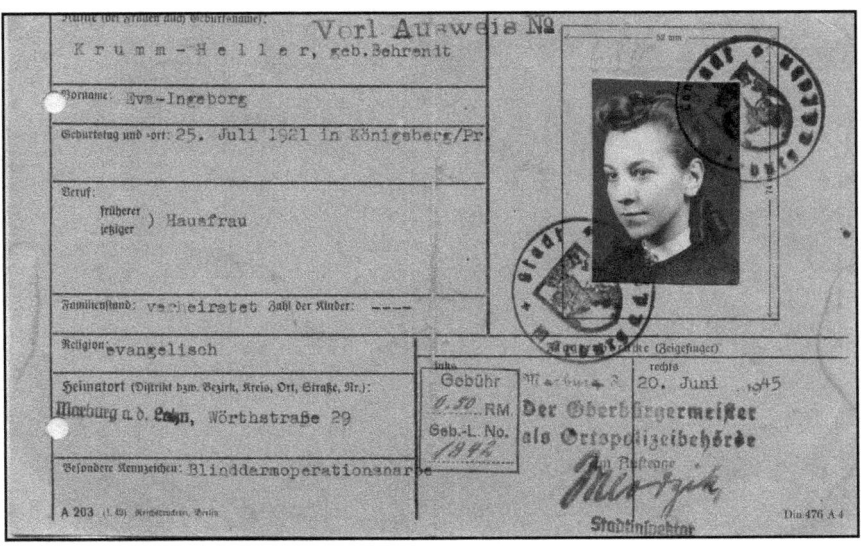

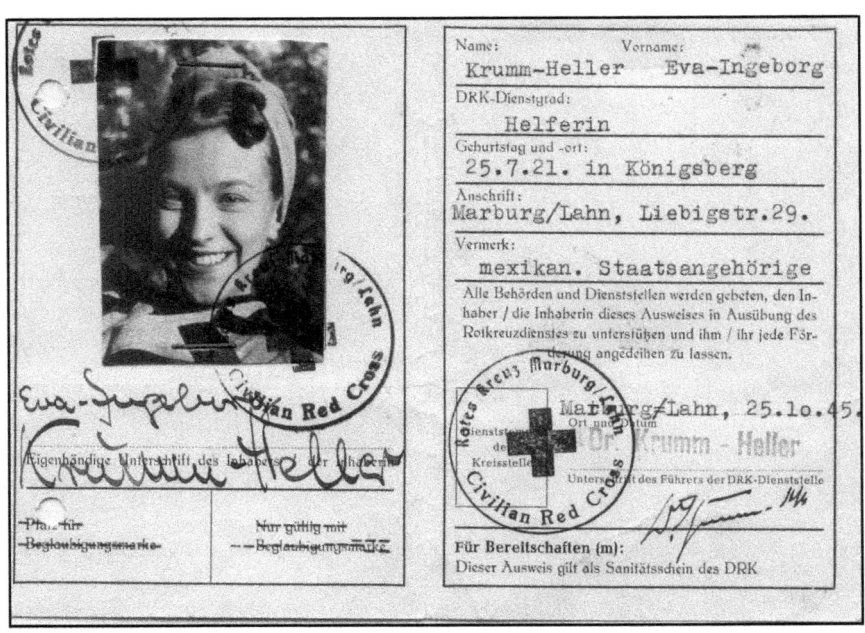

Inge's ID Cards

4

Marburg
July 1945

INGE OPENED HER EYES. It was July 25th, her twenty-fifth birthday. She rolled over and pulled the covers tightly around herself as she thought about the coming day. Her heart leaped with joy and ached of loneliness even though her husband lay next to her. She burrowed deeper into the covers. This was the first of her birthdays as a married woman, but she was still without her mother. She tunneled her legs under the linens to find Moc's cold feet and turned to him. She wanted to lose herself in the warmth of his arms, to forget the sadness she felt. He reached for her, kissed her tenderly, and whispered, "Happy birthday, my love."

Inge and Moc reluctantly got out of bed to face the day. After the wedding, they had moved into Moc's father's house; he lived upstairs. Inge and Moc's section consisted of the small bedroom, a tiny living room, and a makeshift kitchen. Inge looked around at their Lilliputian quarters. As much as she wanted it to, and as much as she tried to make it so, it did not feel like home.

She opened the cupboard and pulled down the two

yellow mugs they had received as a gift from their friend Helmuth and prepared the wonderful black unsweetened coffee. It was a luxury, not to be consumed lightly, but she felt they deserved something special on such a special day.

When the coffee was ready, she called Moc into the living room. He was freshly shaven, his face still damp with aftershave. He used Yardley and she loved it; the aroma soothed and calm her. They sat across from each other. Inge slowly savored the dark and flavorful liquid, letting its warmth glide into her.

Today Inge had the gift of time. She had taken the day off from the photography studio. She couldn't imagine spending her birthday in the darkroom developing photos. She craved the sunlight and didn't want to feel like a mole in a cavern. Moc, on the other hand, had to hurry. He was due at the medical lab. He thought of his work as drudgery and couldn't wait for the day when he and Inge would move to Mexico, where he could make his fortune. He knew Mexico was his destiny and was pleased that he now had Inge as a partner on that journey. He hated the idea of leaving her alone on her birthday, but he had no choice. He would make it up to her tonight.

As he walked out the door, he turned to her and said, "Have a good day, Inge. Relax, enjoy the sunshine, and we'll go out with Helmuth tonight and have a good time."

Inge smiled as the door closed behind him. Although the July day promised to be warm, Inge wrapped her robe more snuggly around her to ward off the bitter cold that seeped into her bones. For months now, she studied the people passing on the streets, hoping against hope to see the face of her mother. She had heard of evacuees from Königsberg and wished her mother was among them, but there were also the horrific stories of Soviet atrocities. Inge couldn't bear the thought of her mother suffering such brutality.

Just like a little girl, Inge longed for her mother on this day. Memories of past birthday celebrations washed over her. She thought about her last birthday before she left for Leipzig, when she was so excited about a new adventure, but now she was consumed by thoughts of how hard it must have been for her mother to let her go. Inge's father was away fighting in the war, Inge was in Leipzig, and her mother was left alone. Regret clutched like a vice at her heart.

She thought of their little house on the outskirts of town, the red roof with its two small chimneys, protruding like two brilliant eyes, permanently etched into her memory. In her mind's eye she climbed the rickety back-porch stairs and stepped into the kitchen, the heart of the home. This was where her mother created her loving offerings. Inge smelled the Königsberg klöße. She heard the faint barking of her beloved long-haired dachshund, Sisi, eagerly waiting to steal droppings.

Her mother laughed. "Get that dog out of here. She keeps scurrying around, and I'm going to trip."

Inge's mother's bulk made it hard for her to move,

and Sisi could easily cause an accident. Inge picked up the dog, nuzzled her, and whispered into her ear,

"Don't worry; I will save you a klöße."

Her mother overheard this and smiled as she dished out the big meatballs smothered in thick white sauce. Inge's mouth watered, and she could taste the comforting mustard flavor, the taste of home.

When they finished their meal, her mother reached for a small square box that she had hidden behind the table.

"I have a special gift for you."

Inge excitedly unwrapped the package, and her eyes widened in astonishment to find a pair of earrings. She held them close to her eyes. Each one cradled two small pearls surrounded by tiny diamonds. The stones were arranged in leaflike patterns and Inge thought they were elegant. They were dainty and delicate and reminded her of images from the fashion magazines she adored. She knew these earrings would be precious to her; they represented her mother's love. She tenderly wrapped her arms around her mother's substantial body and kissed her with gratitude.

Returning from her daydream, Inge wiped a tear from her cheek and finished preparing for her birthday without her mother. She was glad she was home alone because she never let anyone see her cry. Inge pushed down her swelling emotions and combed her hair. She styled the chignon she'd been wrestling with for a few months. Inge didn't like her hair, but it seemed like the proper note for a newly married doctor's wife. This hairstyle went against the elegance that she struck with friends, but, with the last hairpin secured, she solemnly put on her mother's earrings, looked at herself in the mirror, and was satisfied with the image.

There was a knock at the door. Inge was surprised to find an older woman at the threshold, her intense face deeply wrinkled, betraying pain and heartbreak, each crease holding its own story of sorrow and anguish. However, despite the suggestion of sadness, the woman's face bloomed into a brilliant, hopeful smile when they made eye contact. She handed her an envelope and said,

"I am so glad I found you. My name is Helga, and I know your mother."

Inge's parents

Inge's father

Inge's house outside Königsberg

5

Marburg
July 1945

INGE TOOK THE ENVELOPE and looked to the woman in disbelief.

"Your mother knew I was coming to Marburg and asked me to bring this to you. Now I have to be off, I'm late already, but be grateful, child, that your mother is safe and is waiting to see you again." And with that, Helga bid Inge farewell and scurried away down the street.

Inge took a seat in the front room and held her breath as she read the short letter, written in her mother's familiar hand.

My dear child, I love you very much, and I am happy to let you know I was able to leave Königsberg on the last ship before the Red Army invasion. I am staying with a friend in Halle. I have heard nothing from your father. I don't know where he is.

The letter was the best birthday present Inge could have received. As she read and re-read the note, Moc arrived to surprise her for lunch. Inge handed him the note. She hadn't been able to put it down since she received it.

Moc read the letter and said, in his logical and sensible way, "We will go and find your mother."

The next day, without too much planning, they set out. Inge packed a few sandwiches, some clothes, and they left for the train station. Moc's birthday gift to Inge was the train ride to find her mother.

They sat together. As Inge glanced out the window at the passing scenes of ruin, something inside of her jarred loose, and she had to avert her eyes. She was shocked by what she saw. It was impossible to ignore the aftermath of the war and to miss the debris and broken buildings. Like the wrinkles on Helga's face, each one told a tale of dreams extinguished, families broken, lives destroyed.

She tried to focus on the other travelers. Across from her was a mother wrestling with three little boys. They were stairsteps in age and reminded Inge of her three cousins, Frank, Gerhart, and Manfred. She traveled back in time and explored the nooks of her memory, summers at the Baltic Sea, walking the promenade with her aunt and the three boys. Rather than the acrid smells of the train car, it was the slight salty aroma of brackish surf that filled her nostrils.

She remembered feeling grown up in a delicate silky white dress that flowed as she strolled along the promenade. Her shoes had a hint of a heel, but they pinched her toes and she couldn't decide if they were worth the pain. Inge thought of long days playing at the water's edge. She and the boys would perform plays about being pirates lost at sea. A comical image of herself wearing a pirate's hat appeared in her mind and brought a smile to her lips.

The train lurched to a halt and Inge catapulted out of her reverie. Finally, after three days of exhaustive travel, Inge and Moc arrived near Halle. Inge was shocked at the devastation of the city after two recent bombings. She worked hard to control the rising anticipation as they looked for the house where her mother's friend lived, but the excitement was mounting. It had been four years since she'd seen her mother and so much had happened in both their lives. Inge could scarcely wait to tell her all about Henri and Moc and her experiences with the Americans. She also wanted to hear about her beloved Königsberg and how her mother had managed to escape.

When they found the house, they rang the bell, sounding the dull buzzer. The door cracked open. A small gray-haired woman peeked out through suspicious eyes.

I don't blame her for not trusting us, thought Inge. *Trusting anyone in these times is difficult.*

She must have been scared by the vision of two young people, exhausted and dirty from travel. But, of course, everyone in Halle was exhausted and dirty.

"Hello. I'm Inge Behrendt. This is my husband, Moc Krumm-Heller. I understand my mother Franziska Behrendt is here." Suspicion melted from the woman's face, replaced by an emotion Inge could not read.

She opened the door wide and invited them in.

"Oh Inge." She embraced Inge and her voice quavered. "You have just missed your mother." The woman let her go and looked at her through teary eyes.

"I'm afraid she left yesterday."

Inge struggled to grasp what she heard. She had come so close to reaching her mother, and now these words filled her ears like a rush of water.

The woman went on to say, "Your mother got word that your father was captured by the British and is being held at a detention center. She hired a man with a horse and buggy and went to find him."

The weight of the words sank into her, pulling her down, like she had fallen into the ocean and couldn't swim to the surface. She felt like she was drowning. The image of her mother had been like a life preserver that was almost within reach, and now it was gone. Despite Inge's efforts to mask her emotions, Moc sensed her profound disappointment. In his inimitable way, he refused to let a new obstacle deter him. He was single-minded, and when he saw a goal, he tenaciously kept going until he achieved it. He stubbornly concluded,

"We will follow your mother's trail, and we will find her."

The woman told Inge that her mother had received a letter from Inge's father explaining details about the detention camp. Since the war was over, the camp was less harsh. In fact, it was a small isolated village that had been sealed off from the surrounding area and he was living in the home of a Mr. Brant, a local teacher.

Inge and Moc weren't sure of her mother's route, but it the detention camp was run by the British then it was obviously in the British occupation sector, probably somewhere near Düsseldorf. Although still exhausted from the three-day rail journey, they set out on their new quest right away. This time, however, there were no trains that would carry them to their destination.

They set out on foot, tired and hungry. The trip was taking so much longer than Moc and Inge expected but, one step at a time, they would get there. Inge's shoes were muddy and her skirt covered in dust. She was reaching the end of her endurance. She needed a break.

A foreign military truck trundled by. Inge's stomach knotted, and she felt the bile rise in her throat. The war was over, but army vehicles still brought a sense of dread. She thought of the horrible behavior of the Red Army in Königsberg. The devastation around her—and her awareness of the sorts of things that could still happen to German civilians so soon after the war—reminded her that the dangerous times hadn't passed. The western allies didn't seem as harsh as the Soviets, but she still didn't know what a group of soldiers might do, especially to a woman. The truck seemed to be British. It didn't have German emblems on it or an American flag.

Inge heard the the truck stop behind her and her fear increased. *Why did they stop? Would they be safe?* They heard someone call out *guten tag* in phonetic German. Inge and Moc turned to look. The driver leaned out the window and, in Moc's limited English, he understood him to say, "Do you want a ride?" Moc was hesitant. He saw the exhaustion in Inge's eyes, but he also sensed her anxiety. Moc knew they couldn't walk much longer and that curfew would soon descend. He made an impulsive decision.

"Yes, please."

They climbed into the back of the canvas-covered truck and were horrified to find it filled with British soldiers. Inge felt the fear creep up her legs like ants. Nonetheless, she followed Moc into the truck. Like always, Inge worked hard to suppress any visible sign of what was going on inside her. She knew her face had turned white and she could feel the clamminess in her palms. However, she somehow knew that she and Moc would be okay. After all, the war had been over for a few months now, and the Allies had won. She figured they might look with kindness upon a young German couple just walking along the road.

Inge and Moc sat at the back of the truck and tried to be as inconspicuous as they could. Inge's breathing was rapid and shallow, but she worked hard to relax and control it. She closed her eyes and tried to will herself asleep. The soldiers paid little attention. They were tired too, and, like Inge, were trying to asleep. They drove several hours in silence.

As the sun sank in the late afternoon, the truck halted at a cafe and the soldiers piled out. Inge and Moc sat in the in the back and waited for them to return. Inge craned her head around to see what was happening. The British soldiers had stopped for tea. *Of course.*

Thirty minutes later they returned in single file

and climbed back aboard. The first two held cups of tea which they handed to Inge and Moc in turn. Each of the remaining men placed a piece of cake in Inge's lap. She was overcome with appreciation. She and Moc hadn't eaten anything in so long. Now, for the first time, she dared to glance at the soldiers and nod a grateful smile. Inge had experienced American compassion, and now she was the recipient of British kindness.

The remainder of the trip passed in peace and contentment. Inge allowed the movement of the truck to lull her to sleep. While she slept, Moc completed a significant business transaction: He noticed one of the soldiers staring at his wrist. *Could he be coveting his German Junghans watch?*

Moc sensed that he could make a deal. The best currency at the time was cigarettes. In his limited English, he asked the soldier if he was interested in buying his watch with British Dunhill cigarettes in payment. When the soldier agreed, Moc believed he had made a lucrative trade because cigarettes were as good as gold and there were other ways to tell time. After the transaction, Moc and the soldier had a brief conversation. The soldier told Moc the location of the detention center where Inge's father was likely held, but the truck wasn't going there. When they got as close to the center as they were going to get, the truck stopped to let Moc and Inge continue their journey alone.

It was getting late; curfew was approaching. They needed to find a place to safely spend the evening and prepare for the continuation of their journey the next day.

Down the road, they spotted a small inn. The pristine, well-kept building seemed out of place among the destruction that surrounded them. They couldn't imagine how it had escaped the onslaught of the war. It was cared for and cherished. Inge felt it was a safe place to spend the night.

Just as the building's appearance had promised, the proprietors were kind and sympathetic and they welcomed the tired couple with the best hospitality they could muster. Hans, the innkeeper, welcomed them into the cozy front room filled with furniture that was old but meticulously clean. Shelves filled with books and small ceramic figurines lined the walls and bracketed a fireplace that had been swept free of every mote of ash. Only the blackened lining betrayed the fact that the fireplace saw any use at all. Hans patted his hands on the backs of two chairs. He was short and old and wore tiny round glasses. Tufts of gray hair stuck out from his head in every direction. Inge thought he looked just like a troll from a Black Forest tale by the Brothers Grimm. "Please, have a seat and make yourselves comfortable. You have had a long journey, I can tell, and you must refresh yourselves." Hans made a show of wafting air toward his nose and sniffed loudly. "Do you smell that? That is your supper, and my wife makes only one kind of supper: a *superb* one. Please, make yourselves at home, and we will call you to join us at the table."

Inge and Moc awakened to the sound of three hand claps. "Supper is ready, my friends! Else, Hans's wife, helped them to their feet as Inge smoothed out her wrinkled clothing and tried to make herself presentable. "Oh, don't worry about that, dear. Travel is not the friend of glamour and we've seen far worse than you two, so don't trouble yourselves." Else was short and rotund, her hair held back in a dark-blue kerchief, the perfect fairy-tale compliment to Hans. She served them goulash on boiled potatoes. The meat was tender in a delicious, thick, brown cream sauce. Inge loved anything on potatoes, and she felt the pang of longing for her mother who knew just what foods she loved best. Else and Hans listened in awe as Inge and Moc shared the tale of their recent adventures.

Hans badly wanted to help Inge find her father. "Let me see here. I think I have… Ah, yes, I thought I still had a phone directory. It's from 1943. They didn't print one in 1945. But maybe it will be of some use to us." They scanned the names on the onion-skin pages. To Inge's amazement there was a listing for Mr. Brant, the teacher with whom her father was reportedly living.

Inge apprehensively took the receiver from Else's eager hands. She didn't expect to reach her father, but she dialed anyway. Else smiled her approval.

A gentle male voice answered.

"Guten Tag, Herrn Brent hier."

Inge said, "I am Inge Behrendt and I am looking for my father, Gustav. I heard he might be staying there."

After a short pause, Inge heard the tentative and incredulous voice of her father.

"Inge, what are you doing here?"

Inge could hear the emotion in his voice, and it matched the tears that welled in her eyes.

She answered, "I am looking for you and Mutti. Is she there too?"

"No, but I heard from her and she is on her way."

Inge felt joy at the possibility of being reunited with her parents. She said, "Vati, I will come to where you are."

Her father's response impacted Inge to her core.

"My darling, this is the first time in my life there is nothing I can do for you."

The statement made her body go cold. He had always been there to help her, to ease her pain, to clear her path. And now he was powerless. It broke her heart to hear the defeat in his words.

Hans and Else were enchanted by the romance of their story and were as excited as Inge and Moc. They were touched by the idea that Inge had found her father, but he didn't yet know that she was married. They imagined the moment that she would introduce Moc, and her happy reunion with her family. Else wanted Inge to look presentable for the occasion so she showed Inge where she could take a shower, and rummaged through her closet to find some appropriate clothes.

Inge tried on a black pleated skirt. It was too big and too short for her, but with a little creative tucking and wrapping she was able to make it work. She also tried on a couple of Else's blouses and settled on one with pink and orange flowers that matched the joy she felt.

While Inge got ready, Hans and Moc crafted a plan. Hans told Moc the detention center was located across a channel of water to keep it isolated from the neighboring community. Because he lived in town, Hans knew a "big secret." He whispered to Moc,

"Each day, before sunrise, the soldiers ferry people across the channel in a rubber boat—for a fee, of course."

Suddenly the cigarettes that Moc had bartered from the British soldier were burning a hole in his pocket. He knew they would be useful. Now was the time.

The next morning was damp, the dew rising from the water and settling on their clothes. Inge and Moc headed out before the sun peeked over the horizon and quietly walked toward the edge of the channel and waited. Before long a rubber dinghy manned by two soldiers approached by the shore. Inge's apprehension twitched inside her like a fish trying to get off the hook. She had never imagined herself in such a strange situation—sitting on the edge of a channel secretly waiting for soldiers to ferry her across, utterly at their mercy. She reminded herself that on the other side she could finally see her father again.

Moc bargained with the soldiers who seemed happy to negotiate with cigarettes. They settled into the dinghy as it bobbed on the water. Inge was afraid she would fall in.

Moc squeezed her hand and gave her a comforting look. "You are okay; I'll hold on to you. We'll be fine crossing the channel."

The two soldiers ignored Inge and Moc as they paddled the water. It didn't take more than twenty minutes, and to Inge's surprise and relief, they arrived at the other side of the channel safe and sound. Moc exited the dingy and helped Inge step out. Once she was on firm land Inge smoothed down her borrowed clothes and tucked her hair back in place. She felt she looked presentable enough to see her father.

They walked into the small compound. Inge wasn't sure what she had expected, but it wasn't this. It was nothing more than an ordinary town. The houses were well kept, and except for the occasional British soldier, the scene looked like everyday life. The aromas of baking bread and strong coffee permeated the streets. It was hard to believe that this was a detention camp. Inge and Moc knew the house number of the schoolteacher, Mr. Brant, and they soon found his home.

Inge's father stepped out of the front door holding a watering can. Inge saw the surprise in his eyes.

"Peterchen!"—he had called her that since she was a girl—"I can't believe you are here. How did you get here?"

Along with his surprise, she also saw the tenderness and love she had always felt from him. He had always been a small, slight man, but she could tell he had lost weight. As she hugged him, she sensed a frailty that hadn't been there before. She kissed his bald head, their custom since she was a child.

"Vati, I will tell you all about it. I have so much to talk to you about."

She could feel her father peering around her, examining Moc, who stood back. Inge recognized his questioning gaze. *Who is this man with my daughter? Why has he come with her?*

Inge stepped aside. She knew that this was a moment she would remember for the rest of her life. She took a deep breath, stood tall, and said,

"Vati, I would like you to meet my husband, Moc."

Her father's face lit up with joy, and the sparkle in his eyes brought so much emotion to Inge that tears welled within her. He immediately embraced Moc and said, "Children, come inside."

When the three of them entered the living room, Inge was pleased to see a warm place. She had expected her father's captivity would be in a prison-like setting, not in pleasant surroundings with overstuffed furniture. Inge's father introduced them to Mr. Brant, who was cooking in the kitchen. His home had been acquired by the British as a holding facility.

Sitting back in the living room, Inge described their adventure crossing the channel. The question on everyone's mind was: *Where is Mutti?*

Inge's father told them that the last letter he got from her said she was on her way. She planned to hire a horse and buggy to get to the detention camp.

Moc, ever-the-logical one, said, "Well, that means she has to come down the same road we traveled to get here. I will go back with the rubber boat, borrow a bicycle, and go back the same way we came to look for her." Inge gave him a photo so he would recognize her. Per Inge's request, he would not tell her who he was, only that he had been sent to retrieve her and escort her to her husband's temporary home. He knew Inge wanted to be the one to share the surprise of their marriage.

The next morning Moc reversed his steps, exhilarated by the challenge as he waited for the dinghy.

On their first trip across the channel, Moc had noticed a small shed containing some rickety bicycles. He planned to borrow one and pedal back on the road they had traveled only yesterday until he caught up with Inge's mother.

Moc was pleased with his luck. All went as he expected. The soldiers gladly accepted more cigarettes, and the bicycle waited for him in the shed. Moc began pedaling. The heavy morning dew descended on him, and beads of sweat accumulated on his forehead. He wondered what impression he would make when he introduced himself to his mother-in-law.

He didn't have to wonder long. After half an hour of strenuous pedaling, he came upon a horse towing a buggy. The driver was a bearded man with fierce, penetrating eyes. Inside was a portly, elegant woman. Moc recognized her immediately as the one in the photo he carried his breast pocket.

Moc flagged down the driver who gave him an intense squint. A sense of unease percolated in Moc about the man, but he ignored it. His goal was to connect with his mother-in-law, and that's what he would do. He reached inside the buggy and extended his hand. "Frau Behrendt?" Moc sensed her suspicion. He imagined her thoughts. *A man I don't know stops me on the road and knows my name. That is terrifying.*

She offered a tentative "Yes?"

Moc smiled warmly to put her at ease. "I come from your husband and your daughter who are waiting for you at the detention center."

"My daughter?" she said incredulously, but Moc heard the delight in her voice.

"I will take you to them, but we must spend the night at the inn down the street and then cross a channel in the morning."

Hans and Else's eyes grew wide when they saw Moc and Inge's mother arrive in the buggy. Hans took Moc aside and asked,

"Where did you find this driver? Do you know he is the escapee from a mental hospital? The authorities have been looking for him for weeks."

When they returned to look for the driver he had already moved on. Hans and Else called the authorities to let them know. Moc was grateful nothing had happened. He dismissed the incident and felt it was just another colorful event during this adventure, a story that he would one day share with his children.

They spent the night with Else and Hans, Moc having given them a conspiratorial glance warning them not to divulge the secret of his identity and spoil Inge's surprise.

Inge's mother was still suspicious. Moc saw the narrowing of her eyes and her curious glances. At dinner, she finally confronted him with questions. *Who are you? Why are you traveling with my daughter? I see you have a wedding ring.*

Moc was prepared for this and he spun a tale of friendship and support. He sensed his mother-in-law did not fully believe him, but she was too polite to challenge his story.

The next morning, Moc retraced his steps again and was astounded that his supply of cigarettes was enough for one more trip. The passing on the channel was more difficult with Inge's mother. Her weight lowered the dingy into the water to the point that it threatened to pour over the edge. Moc sensed her fear and watched her face turn ashen. Her hand trembled as she grasped his arm, but he smiled reassuringly as they arrived safely at the other edge. Moc felt her wobbly legs and buckling knees as he helped her step on the firm ground.

Together they walked the short distance to Mr. Brant's house. The closer they got, the stronger Moc's anticipation grew.

When they arrived, Moc smiled internally at his role as Inge's knight in shining armor for having found her parents. He was not disappointed. When he saw the joy in Inge's face at their reunion he knew it had all been worth it.

Moc stood back and absorbed the warmth surrounding Inge's parents' embrace when they reached for their daughter.

Then Inge extended her hand to Moc and brought him into the family circle.

Inge stepped out of the embrace. Once again, she stood tall and allowed the pride to fill her heart as she said,

"Mutti, I want to introduce you to my husband, Cuauhtémoc Krumm-Heller."

INES ROE

Inge's mother with Sisi the dog

Inge's father

Inge's aunt and her cousins walking on the Promenade in Kranz on the Baltic Sea.

Part II

...Of Ordinary

6

MARBURG
SEPTEMBER 1945

INGE SMILED. THINGS WERE good now that she was reunited with her parents. It was a reset to gentle normalcy. The war was over, and she was easily lulled into a new routine. After the reunion and her father's release, everyone returned to Marburg to resume life there. Inge and Moc prepared for a festive family dinner at her parents' new apartment.

Mutti had been lucky to get a job as a cook at an art school. Tonight, she would show off her talents to her new son-in-law by cooking their first home-cooked meal as a family. Inge hoped it would be her delicious goulash.

Her parents' safety filled Inge with more gratitude than she could express. But it also came with a sense of loss of the life she had known. Her mother was with them now in Marburg because she had successfully fled the Soviet invasion of Königsberg. Inge wasn't sure she wanted to hear the story of the escape, but she knew her mother needed to share it. Tonight would be her mother's occasion to share her ordeal. Inge and Moc arrived at the cozy apartment that her parents had rented. After sharing embraces, Inge realized now how much they had aged and what a toll the war had taken on them. They sat on the lumpy flowered couch they had bought from a family who left Germany for the Philippines. Inge looked around the space at the welcome sight of items she remembered from her childhood. On the table were two silver candlesticks Inge knew belonged to her grandparents. They were precious to her mother because they were among the few things she still had from her own parents. She also saw the bright gold-colored amber box. Amber was special to her family because it was a symbol of Königsberg, the greatest amber producer in the world. There were a few family photos scattered around. Inge wondered how her mother had managed to rescue these family treasures and carry them with her on such a perilous journey.

Mutti watched as Inge's eyes roamed across the apartment. She tried to imagine what was going through her mind. She knew she had many questions about what happened in Königsberg, but she wasn't yet ready to tell her story.

At the dinner table, Mutti ladled meat chunks smothered in creamy brown gravy over the noodles. Inge's mouth watered as the sights and smells flooded her with memories of earlier times. She could almost feel the soft fur of their dog Sisi brushing against her leg. She smiled, imagining that her parents shared the same memory. The meal warmed her heart and her stomach. As Mutti went to the kitchen to bring the pound cake dessert to the table, Inge sensed she was fortifying herself for her account. And indeed, after serving a slice to each of them, she began.

"I want to tell you about my last few days in Königsberg and how I escaped. It is something I'd rather forget, but I can't until I tell you about it and unburden my soul. I thank God I was lucky to be one of those who escaped." A mixture of revulsion and fear crept into Inge's stomach. She needed to hear her mother's tale of escape, but she feared that it was filled with horrible things that she would rather not know. Still, she *needed* to know. She glanced at her father and saw helplessness and resignation at what was to come.

Mutti continued, "In August we survived a four-day bomb attack by the British. It destroyed a large part of the city and killed thousands of people. Then we heard of the massacre by Red Army soldiers in Nemmersdorf. Women, young girls, and even old women like me were raped. There were stories about naked women crucified on barn doors. Frau Becker, you remember our neighbor, and I sat by the radio each night hearing the reports. We were not sure what we were supposed to do—were we to stay or were we to flee? We were alone, and frightened." Inge felt a pang of guilt when she heard this. Would things have been different had she stayed with her? Would she have been able to help her mother feel less frightened?

Mutti's face had turned pale. "We couldn't decide what to do, but the Red Army was very close and we knew we would have to do something soon. Then the evacuation order came. It was so difficult for Frau Becker and me to leave but we knew we had no choice. There were others in the neighborhood who were leaving too. Once we made the decision there was little time. I grabbed the few family mementos that you see around you. I didn't know if I would ever see you again, and I wanted to preserve our memories." Inge felt the tears spill out as she looked at the photographs of her childhood. She imagined the agony her mother must have felt at having to make such difficult choices—what to take and what to leave behind—and embarking into an uncertain future.

"We walked to the train station, each of us with a small suitcase. All along the road were discarded items people couldn't carry anymore—embroidered pillowcases and tablecloths, children's toys, engraved tableware, things that were obviously family heirlooms, abandoned on the side of the road. No one picked any of it up; we were all too desperate to leave. At the station everything was confusion. Massive amounts of people pushing and shoving to get on the train. Mothers were comforting wailing babies and children were vomiting in the street. It was chaos, but we knew we had to get on the train.

"I was breathless and dizzy. There were people hanging on the edge of the train and men sitting on the roof. I don't remember ever being so terrified. You could hear the guns in the distance; everyone was panicking, desperate to escape. It seemed I couldn't be fast enough to squeeze in. I thought I wouldn't make it. Then a kind man held my hand and pulled me aboard. Thankfully, Frau Becker and I made it on the train."

Mutti grew quiet, and the family felt the tension in the

room as she assembled the memories in her mind. The flow became a deluge as she spoke of the crushing fear she experienced. "I could do nothing but trust that God would care for me and lead me to safety. The train was destined to the shore at Pillau. We were told to board a ship and we would be taken to Danzig. I watched passengers whisper with grim faces. Frau Becker and I wondered what they spoke about. She had the courage to ask, and what she learned terrified us." Mutti closed her eyes. Inge remembered the story of a previous refugee ship, the Wilhelm Gustloff, which months earlier sank from Soviet torpedoes, taking the lives of almost 10,000 evacuees. "Frau Becker and I sat and prayed together for the entire voyage. I clutched my little suitcases with my mementos. I feared this was all I would have of you."

Inge felt the anguish in her mother's voice when she described the ordeal of arriving at the port and boarding the ship that would take them to Danzig. She wanted to stop listening as she described the trek up the plank and into the hold. Inge could tell that her mother was still disturbed by the memory of being confined in the overcrowded ship, overcome by nausea and claustrophobia, always wondering if they were about to be sunk to the bottom.

Mutti ended her story abruptly. It was clear she didn't want to think about it anymore. She quickly described their arrival in Danzig and how she and Frau Becker found their way to Halle, concluding with a happy ending despite the hardship.

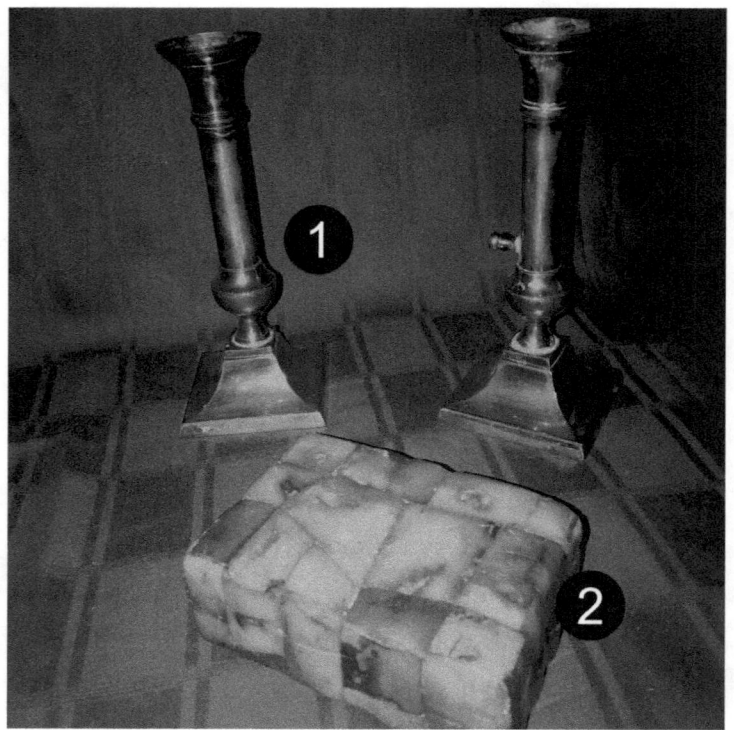

Items Inge's mother was able to bring from Königsberg.
1) silver candle sticks
2) Amber box

7

Paris
December 1945

INGE REACHED FOR THE nightstand, fumbled around blindly for a moment, found the alarm clock, and turned it off. She opened her sleepy eyes and realized with horror that she hadn't set it correctly.

Inge shook Moc awake in a panic. "We need to get up or we'll miss the train!" Thank goodness they had packed everything for their journey to Paris the night before. All they had to do was throw on some clothes and grab the suitcases.

They frantically ran down the stairs and found Helmuth standing by his car. "I was getting worried about you two. I was on my way up to make sure you were awake." Moc nodded, but Inge could see the worry etched in his face. They were going to Paris to get Moc's passport renewed. They couldn't do it in Marburg because there was no Mexican consulate there. Paris was the closest one and their journey to Mexico was impossible without a valid passport.

Isabella was waiting for them at the station. She bit her lower lip as she anxiously scanned the crowd. A slow, tentative smile appeared when Inge and Moc stepped into view. Inge could tell she recognized Moc.

Isabella was tall. Her lanky body reminded Inge of the Venus de Milo. She wore a long white cashmere coat that Inge thought was the most beautiful thing she had ever seen. She wanted to touch it and feel its softness. She could only imagine the warmth of wearing such a beautiful and luxurious thing. Inge had never met Isabella but she knew about her. She was from Chile and, according to Moc, she spoke only broken German. Her husband, one of Moc's friends, had asked if they would escort her to Paris so she could go to the bank to collect the money her parents sent to her from Chile.

Moc walked up to Isabella and kissed her hand. "Inge, I would like you to meet Isabella. We will accompany her to Paris." The two women smiled at each other warmly, and Inge knew they could be friends. After all, they would be sharing the next ten hours and six hundred kilometers together with little to do but talk and nap.

Moc helped the two women into the cabin. The crowded train made it difficult to find adjacent seats. They settled across from an older woman who was busily digging into her large purse. Inge was immediately captivated by her fingernails. They were long, slightly rounded, and painted a glossy red. Inge's own nails were a wreck; she bit them when she was nervous, and she had been nervous a lot lately. Looking at the lady's elegant hands, Inge vowed that one day she would care for her nails and polish them the same way.

Moc instantly fell asleep, and the three women began

to chat. Inge was interested in finding out more about her two traveling companions. Isabella shared that she grew up in Chile and her parents lived in Santiago, the capital. She met her husband when he visited as a representative for the Siemans Company. They fell in love, and her parents gave her permission to marry and follow him to Germany. In broken German, Isabella said, "It has been hard for me. I miss Chile, and I didn't know what Germany was like. I was scared about the war, and I am so happy it is over. I hope Hans will be willing to move back to Chile now."

Inge smiled at the older woman with the fancy nails. She introduced herself as Brigitte. She was a widow; her husband died before the war began. "My parents were French, and I live on the border between France and Germany. I often travel back and forth. It's complicated for me because the Germans don't like the French and the French don't like the Germans. I often feel caught in the middle."

By that time Moc began to stir and was glad to join the conversation. Inge and Moc were pleased to share their story of finding Inge's parents and how happy they were to be moving on with their plans to move to Mexico. Moc shared his experience with the American occupation and buying the occupation money which financed their trip to France. Inge watched Brigitte's face turn sorrowful. "Oh kids, you are mistaken. That money is worthless in France. The occupation money in France is different. So, you have no money." She was so kind and sympathized with their sudden plight. She said, "But, you know, I live on the border. I can use both. I will buy some of your German money with French money."

Inge and Moc were astonished at their situation, and grateful they met Brigitte to help them. When they arrived at the Paris station, they had to make a new plan. They said goodbye to Brigitte, thanking her for saving them, and helped Isabella with her luggage.

"Well," Moc said, "we have to make some adjustments to our plans. We have a lot less money than we thought. The first thing we have to do is find a place to stay. We have enough for one night in a hotel." They found one right across from the train station. It was called the Grand Hotel, but Inge instantly saw it was far from grand. The outside walls were grimy and stained. She imagined that it might have been a luxurious hotel many years ago, but certainly not today.

When they entered the lobby Inge absurdly worried about Isabella's beautiful white cashmere coat. She realized how ridiculous this thought was, but it encapsulated the distaste she felt. Tears pooled in her eyes, but she knew she couldn't show how appalled she was that they would be spending the night in this place.

A man she assumed was drunk sat on the floor in a corner snoring. The sour stench of body odor and cigarette smoke sprung from the walls. The threadbare carpet was packed with dust and mud drug in on countless shoes. Inge thought, *If this is the lobby, I can only imagine what the rooms are like.* But she braced herself and smiled.

When Inge and Moc walked into their room, it was just the way Inge imagined it would be: dingy and grimy. But it would have to do for the night. It was late, and they needed to get some sleep before the next day's trek to the Mexican consulate. Moc looked at Inge and said, "I am so sorry. I know this isn't what we imagined, but I promise you it will get better."

Inge had to go to the bathroom and realized it was down the hall, shared with the other guests. She was terrified to go by herself. As much as she tried to avoid the image, all that came to her was the memory of the movie *Frankenstein*. She feared the monster was lurking in a dark corner and would spring out. Moc walked her down the hall and waited with her. No monsters would attack tonight.

Although they were exhausted from the trip, they had a hard time falling asleep. Inge heard every noise. She could hear the loud French voices arguing in the room next door as well as the crawling of the roaches she saw in the corner.

Early the next morning they met Isabella in the lobby. She looked like she hadn't slept at all, and Inge could understand. At least she had Moc to protect her. They accompanied her to the Chase Manhattan Bank so she could collect the money her parents had sent from Chile.

Afterward, Moc and Inge set out to find the Mexican consulate. Moc only had the address, and he spoke little French. They decided to walk since the map showed it wasn't too far away and they couldn't afford carfare. Inge was excited about being in Paris. She tried to forget the horrible night in the hotel and instead focus on the mythical elegance of the City of Light. She could see the Eiffel Tower in front of them, the very symbol of culture and grace. Inge knew that France was the global center of haute couture and she wanted to soak in the glamour. But she couldn't help but have mixed feelings. Only one year ago the French had been liberated from her countrymen and she wondered if she would be accepted as a German.

When they arrived at the consulate, Inge saw Moc straighten shoulders and back. He held his head up, confidently walked into the anteroom, stopped at the receptionist, and proudly said, "Hello, my name is Cuauhtémoc Krumm-Heller, and I am here to renew my Mexican passport. I would like to see the consul general." The receptionist smiled kindly and said, "Oh, I am so sorry, the consul general is not here this week. You can meet with his deputy, Señor Esparza." She took Moc's passport and escorted them into the office.

The office was large and imposing. Inge saw the Mexican flag behind the desk. She had never seen it. It was a green, white, and red tricolor, like Italy's, but instead of the arms of the House of Savoy in the center it had an emblem of an eagle eating a serpent. Inge was appalled by the image.

She watched the man behind the massive oak desk pick up Moc's passport. He had a large build that seemed to overflow his chair; his dark, limp mustache hung over his lips like a drawn curtain. Inge saw no warmth or kindness; on the contrary, she sensed contempt. He turned his chair to the side, and tightened his lower jaw. Inge didn't know what was happening, but she didn't have a good feeling. Finally he said, "Krumm-Heller?" Turning to the receptionist, he said, "Ask these people to leave my office."

Inge and Moc were shocked. They didn't know how to respond, and they were ushered out of the office before they could protest. Inge could tell the receptionist was stunned too. Under her breath, she whispered to Moc, "Come back in two weeks. The consul will be back, and you shouldn't have a problem then."

As they left the consulate, they felt stunned and lost. They could not understand the rebuff and sat on a bench down the street trying to make sense of what had happened. Moc was not an expert in Mexican history, but he knew his father had been a force in Mexican politics. He told Inge as much as he could remember of his father's arrival in Mexico as a grand wizard of Mexican Freemasonry. He forged a relationship with another prominent Freemason, Franciso Madero, a Mexican revolutionist who challenged Porfirio Díaz's re-election to the Mexican presidency in 1910. Madero became known as the "leader of the revolution" and was president after Díaz resigned in 1911. Moc's father became Madero's personal physician in 1911 and secured Mexican citizenship. Madero, however, was assassinated in 1913. Moc said, "I think my father worked for the Military Intelligence Division and he became a 'secret agent' for Venustiano Carranza who was a revolutionary and became the thirty-seventh Mexican president. My father was arrested in 1913 by the Mexican government for being a spy, and he served seventeen days in prison. Maybe the deputy counsel knows my father and doesn't have a good impression of him. It's the only explanation I can think of."

While Inge thought this was all interesting, it didn't solve their immediate problem of being in Paris with no money and no prospects for at least two more weeks. Inge knew she would not be able to spend another night in the Grand Hotel.

They slowly walked back, contemplating their options. When they arrived at the lobby, Isabella was waiting for them. She had returned from the bank and was preparing to return to Germany. She was astounded by their experience at the consulate and tried to help them think of a plan.

She offered a suggestion. "I'm leaving to go back to Germany. I have the money my parents sent me from Chile. I would be happy to lend you some of the money and leave it with you. I know your parents will pay me back when I return to Germany." Inge and Moc were reluctant to take her up on her offer, but they knew they had no other choice.

They accompanied Isabella to the train station with her luggage and helped her board the train. Inge embraced her warmly and was grateful to have such a good friend. She was sorry to see her go.

Now, with the little bit of money they had from Isabella's loan, Moc and Inge found a hotel that was a little nicer—but not much. They had nothing to do but wait the two weeks until the consul returned.

Before they left Marburg many of their friends had given them addresses of friends and acquaintances they knew in Paris. Inge and Moc set out to make "the rounds."

They looked on their map and found the address of some Russian immigrants their friend Gerhard had given them. When they arrived, and shyly rang the bell, they were greeted by an imposing middle-aged woman dressed in an elegant caftan and a bright pink turban who introduced herself as Vetrova. When Moc explained their relationship to Gerhard she invited them inside. Inge was profoundly affected by Vetrova. She was so warm and welcoming. She hugged Inge to her enormous bosom and although she had never met them before she said, "Children, how wonderful to see you."

Moc and Inge felt transported to another country and another century. A long cigarette holder dangled from Vetrova's mouth. Her voice was thick with a heavy Russian accent.

Gerhart had told them that Vetrova was part of a group of White Russians who had escaped Russia before the revolution, and indeed her home was filled to the brim with ornate memorabilia of pre-revolutionary Russia. A photo of Czar Nicholas II and his family was the centerpiece of the room. Further back was a heavy wooden cabinet filled with dolls dressed in colorful and brilliant costumes.

In the corner, a phonograph played Russian folk music. Inge was captivated by the sounds and colors and felt transported to Russia. She could only imagine how sad it must be for Vetrova to know her home no longer existed as she remembered it. Neither did Inge's. The country in which she had lived most of her life was gone and it would never be the same. She understood perfectly how Vetrova must feel, but she also remembered that it was the Russians who devastated Königsberg and forced her mother to flee.

Inge banished these thoughts and instead focused on Vetrova and her imposing character. In her pronounced Russian speech, she said, "Children, I just made a big pot of borscht. Why don't you stay and keep me company?" With so little money, Inge and Moc had not eaten anything that day. They were grateful for the thick red soup and the crusty bread. They ate eagerly.

Vetrova sat back and watched them. She could sense their hunger and wanted to hear their story. Inge and Moc recounted their past few days, telling about the American Occupation money and how little they had left.

Vetrova's face lit up. She pointed to a certificate on the wall and said, "that is what I do when we begin to run out of money." It was a receipt from a pawn shop. This gave them an idea. When they returned to the hotel, Moc took the few pieces of jewelry Inge had and took them to the pawn shop. Moc knew this was hard for Inge. The jewelry was all she had to remind her of home. The pieces were the select few that meant something in the family. She had the ring Henri had given her, Moc's mother's ring and garnet broach, and the diamond earrings from her mother. Inge had been wearing most of them because she hadn't wanted to leave them behind in the hotel. She reluctantly took them off and handed them to Moc. She could tell it broke his heart to take them, and he said "Ingeline, I promise you I will get them back. The money we get from pawning them will hold us over until the consul returns and we get my passport."

Inge waited for him in the hotel lobby. She watched the people entering and leaving. She was fascinated by the characters milling around. A young woman in a heavy coat sat next to her and smiled. Inge didn't speak much French; she remembered only the little she learned in school in Königsberg. She remembered her favorite teacher, Fräuline Floto, an elegant lady who had studied in Paris. Inge waited each day to see what she would wear. She wondered what Fräuline Floto would think of her today, sitting in a Paris hotel using the French she had taught her.

Inge began a conversation with the young woman, *"Bonjour, comment vas-tu?"* Her heavy Germanic accent told the woman that Inge spoke little French. She smiled and introduced herself as Genevieve. She said she spoke a little German. The two began to communicate in their broken languages. Inge talked about their recent experiences in Paris and feeling lost.

Inge learned valuable information from Genevieve. She couldn't wait to tell Moc. She had the solution to their hunger. Genevieve had told her about the United Nations Relief and Rehabilitation Administration, or UNRRA, which was managed by the Americans. After the liberation of Paris, Americans sent "care packages" and gave them to the French to be distributed to displaced people. They also arranged for a type of soup kitchen, also organized by the UNRRA. The menu was always macaroni and cheese for lunch and cabbage soup for dinner which, in Inge's hunger, sounded delicious.

When Inge and Moc walked into the large hall of UNRRA they were bombarded with the sounds, sights, and smells of despair. Inge had to remind herself how much Paris had suffered. She felt guilty because she knew Germany had occupied Paris for over four years and food was still scarce.

She remembered seeing a newspaper photo of the liberation of France. Because she was German she felt she should feel a certain way, but she wasn't sure what it should be. She remembered her bewilderment when she saw the American troops marching into Marburg. How did the French feel when they were liberated from the Germans? Inge was just glad the war was over, and both countries could now begin to rebuild.

The UNRRA hall was crowded and it buzzed like

a busy beehive. Despite the commotion, Inge's eyes were drawn to a corner table. She couldn't look away. Two little children, a boy and a girl, probably eight and ten, blond, the boy with chopped hair reaching into his eyes and a toy car that he rolled along the table. The girl hugged a small stuffed bear. Each had a bowl of macaroni and cheese, and Inge could see their joy as they shoveled the gooey warmth into their mouths. Inge didn't have much experience with children but she was touched by the scene. She could only imagine how they must have been impacted by the events of their short lives.

Inge and Moc got into the line and patiently waited their turn. When they received their bowls of macaroni, Inge thought it was the best thing she had ever eaten. She was familiar with macaroni and cheese, but for her it was known as *Käsespätzle* and reminded her of home. She inhaled the dense aroma and let the cheesy warmth spread through her mouth. She greedily ate as much as she could. Inge was grateful for the food that helped banish her hunger, but eating it launched a new emotion: apprehension. She asked herself, *What is going to happen to us as we sit here and wait?* This is only a temporary solution. She didn't want to tell Moc just how uncertain she felt about what was happening and her fears about what would happen next.

Waiting was all that they could do. Wait until the consul returned to renew Moc's passport. Wait at the hotel and eat the meals provided by the charity of the victors.

Inge and Moc's days began to repeat, one after another, a familiar ritual. Despite the bone weariness of taking the daily walk in the cold, they felt the determination in their mission. They woke up each morning and walked to the Mexican embassy hoping the consul had returned from Berlin. Each day they were frustrated and disappointed. All they could do was to continue their trek to UNRRA to fill their bellies.

They began to recognize the people there and develop friendships. Moc had formed a close relationship with François, one of the cooks. He had broad shoulders from lifting the daily delivery of heavy supply bags. His hands were knobby and twisted, raw from exposure to the scorching stoves and ovens. During his breaks he would find Moc and sit with him to discuss politics and the news.

Each day was colder than the last. Moc had a heavy winter coat, and François envied it. He knew Moc and Inge needed money and offered to buy the coat, but his kindness prevailed. He said, "No, I really can't do that—it's too cold, and I can't leave you without a coat. But I have an idea for you. My girlfriend, Gabriel, works for a wealthy family and she told me they are looking for another maid. Maybe Inge could work for them."

Moc didn't know how Inge would feel about that. She was with a group of friends on the other side of the room. Moc gently pulled her aside and struggled to find the right words. Inge watched his expression change. She couldn't imagine what was going through his mind and she was worried that something terrible had happened and that Moc couldn't quite figure out how to break the news. Rubbing and biting his bottom lip, sheepishly avoiding eye contact, he finally said, "Darling, I know this isn't what I promised you, but I have a temporary plan for us. How would you feel about working as a chambermaid for a family for a while? It would give us a little money to make ends meet."

Inge was surprised Moc had to ask. He should know she would do whatever was necessary for them to achieve their goal. She was excited by the possibility of earning money. She said, "find out the address, and we will go immediately. Maybe I can start today."

The freezing cold penetrated their bones as they walked the few blocks to the family's home. Inge was glad Moc would be able to keep his coat. They double checked the address. The apartment seemed massive. It was three floors with a balcony projecting from the third level. Each story had a wall of windows with green and white awnings. The apartment house lent a cheery appearance to an otherwise bleak street.

The bell was answered by a young woman who introduced herself as Claudette, the cook. With a fluttering, nervous feeling in her stomach, Inge said, "Hello, I am Inge Krumm-Heller and I understand there is an opening for a maid." With a warm smile and a welcoming wink, Claudette told Inge that "Madame" would arrive in a few minutes.

Inge quieted her stomach and was instantly overwhelmed by the grandeur of her surroundings. The open entryway with the high ceilings and massive chandeliers framed a curving stairway. In the middle of the room stood a large glass table with a bouquet of colorful tulips. The aroma assaulted her senses. Inge cautiously surveyed the slate floor. She imagined it would be her task to clean it along with polishing the heavy oak furniture. She felt tired already.

Inge couldn't help but wonder how the family managed to live in such opulence despite the war. Her thoughts ended abruptly as Madame made her entrance, seeming to float above the floor in a massive gown that trailed behind her. Without introducing herself she said, in an aristocratic tone, "What experience have you had cleaning?"

Inge spoke about her mother's expectations and how she had learned to keep a clean home from her. Madame made up her mind quickly. She hired Inge on the spot.

Inge started the same day and began her tasks of washing, ironing, and buffing the wooden furniture. She felt happy to be in a beautiful environment and didn't mind the work, glad to be distracted from the boredom of the past few days and the apprehension of waiting for the next part of their lives to begin.

Inge learned from Claudette that Madame's husband was a high-ranking police officer and they were preparing for a large weekend soiree. Inge took it upon herself to make sure everything was clean and buffed for the party. She loved parties, and she had grown fond of Madame over the past few days and wanted to make sure everything was just right. Madame walked into the cavernous living room and watched as Inge dusted and cleaned. She could see how hard Inge worked and said, "We are going to have so much food left over, why don't you ask your husband to come by after the party."

When Moc picked Inge up that night, she was happy to share her good fortune with him. She said, "Moc, we will have a full belly tomorrow, and it won't be from macaroni and cheese or cabbage soup. Claudette must have told Madame that we're having a difficult time because she invited us to come after the party and have leftovers. Isn't that wonderful?" Moc felt bad that they would have to take "charity" from Madame, but he knew he had to be practical and seize the opportunities that were offered to them.

The night of the party Inge worked hard in the kitchen, helping the servers prepare the trays of canapés, and doing anything else that needed to be done. She enjoyed the glamour of the party and peeked into the salon to see all the elegant guests, hoping that one day she and Moc would host such a fancy and stylish gathering. Inge was excited when Moc arrived. He shared her delight at watching the elegant guests.

As Moc and Inge ate the delicious leftovers that Inge had helped prepare, Madame came into the kitchen. Moc instantly stood up, bowed, and kissed her hand. She greeted him warmly and said, "you know, my husband needs a chauffeur. Do you know how to drive?"

"Yes, Madame."

She said, "Come back tomorrow at ten to meet my husband."

That night, when Inge and Moc returned to the hotel, they felt the tide of their fortunes changing. The next morning, Madame's husband had many questions for Moc. After a while, he said, "well, I can tell you're no chauffeur. Tell me what you *are*."

"I am a doctor, sir."

"In that case, I know someone who could use you. Go and see Professor Bojerone at the Sorbonne."

Moc was nervous that night. It seemed like a unique opportunity. But, at the same time, it changed the course of their plans. If Moc were able to get a job, they could stay in Paris instead of traveling to Mexico. That night, Moc had a dream. He was walking in the woods when he came to a fork in the road. He had to make a decision about which path to take. He told Inge the next morning, "I knew either path had consequences affecting our destiny." He laughed. "I guess it's not too hard to figure out the significance of the dream. The decision we make will alter the course of our lives. What do you think?"

Inge had always planned to live an extraordinary life. She wanted to go places and do things that exceeded the mundane, that surpassed the normal circumstances of simple existence. Paris offered comfort and security, but it wasn't the life that she had wanted. Nonetheless, what could she do? They needed money, food, shelter, all of the things that she had never had to worry much about in the past. Now those were the only things that seemed to matter. She said, "I like Paris. I think we can be happy here."

When Moc came home that evening he told Inge, "Well, I met with Professor Bojerone, and it felt like we had an instant connection." He went on to tell her that Professor Bojerone was consulting at a pharmaceutical company called Teraplix and told Moc, "I need an assistant, and you are the man. You have the job if you want it." Moc announced to Inge with gleaming eyes, "I accepted the job."

Paris
1950s

INGE AND MOC WERE excited. Their life together was about to transform and they began to make plans. Moc said, "If we're going to stay in Paris, we'll need to find a place to live." But, before that happened, they used Moc's first paycheck to assemble a box of French delicatessen to send to Inge's parents. Inge felt great joy at sending the special package and hoped it would entice them to come and visit once they were settled.

With Moc's new income Inge was able to quit her job as Madame's chambermaid and settle into a life in Paris. She was excited about her approaching birthday and wondered what surprises Moc had in store for the celebration.

She wasn't disappointed. On her birthday, she found a huge bowl filled with apples, bananas, and peaches, with a pineapple in the center, on the dinner table. Grapes and cherries, Inge's favorite fruits, were scattered throughout. The colorful arrangement seemed like an extravagant luxury and it filled her with awe to see it. She was stunned and grateful for such a wonderful indulgence. As she embraced Moc, he said, "I know you love fruit and would enjoy the sweet taste, but if you look closer at the bowl there might be another surprise for you." Inge explored the bowl. Tears welled in her eyes when she found what he had hidden. Deeply embedded in the fruit was the jewelry that they had pawned when they were penniless, her priceless family heirlooms that she thought she would never see again. She put on the rings, earrings, and brooches, and felt reconnected to her past and ready to continue towards the future.

Inge and Moc were young, and Paris, even so soon after the war, was a bold and vibrant metropolis. Now that they had a little money they could finally begin to find their place in the City of Light. But the longer they stayed, and the more settled they became, the more Inge felt a creeping unease, a sense of trepidation that she couldn't quite put her finger on, a sensation that this wasn't where she was supposed to be and that something, some other place, was beckoning to her.

They began to meet other young people and attended parties. Inge loved to be elegant and Hilda, one of her new friends, made a skirt for her. Hilda was a seamstress and knew all of the comings and goings of the fashionable set around the city. "I know someone who is opening a millinery. He's looking for girls to help him make hats. I know you don't know how to sew, but wouldn't it be fun for us to work together?" Inge was looking for something different from the photography studio and being stuck in the darkroom, so she tagged along with Hilda one day to meet the milliner, Monsieur Pierre Arbelle. She put on her most stylish clothes (now sadly a little out of date, but no worse than what many other women were wearing in the difficult postwar environment) and gave her best, most radiant smile when she was introduced.

Monsieur Arbelle was short and rotund, dressed in flamboyant colors that marked him as a man of fashion. He took her hand. "Ah, I am so pleased to meet you. Hilda has told me so much. She has also told me that you cannot sew, but not to worry. I can teach you to create the most electrifying hats, such as you have never seen. What I cannot teach is the simple elegance that comes from within, what we see when you move, when you walk, when you smile. And if what Hilda says is true, and if my eyes do not deceive me (and I know that they don't), then you, my dear, are just the person I am looking for." He smiled and touched her nose with the tip of his finger. Inge was speechless.

Hilda took her to the workroom and showed her how the hats were made. "Don't be *too* flattered," she told Inge. "He says something like that to everyone."

At first, Inge and Hilda were the only hired help, but then Monsieur Arbelle hired four more. He also had six brothers who were always busily working on things, so the studio was active every moment of the day. The brothers came and went, and when they returned they often brought champagne from wherever it was they had been. They would sew hats for a while and then sing and dance during their breaks, and of course they needed dance partners. Inge was having a brilliant time, making friends, learning new things, and beginning to feel as though she were becoming a part of the fabric of the city. Monsieur Arbelle was talented and made fantastic hats, but the most wonderful thing was that he allowed Inge to take the hats home. Each night she went home wearing a different, fabulous hat.

They also met an older couple through Moc's work, Madame and Monsieur Bernard. There was only one problem: The Bernards hated Germans. The French held such a hatred toward the Germans at that time that Inge feared telling anyone where she was from. She had always been a proud German, but she also understood perfectly why there was so much animosity. Although they realized that it was dishonest, they felt it would be better for everyone to present Inge as Swedish.

One evening, when they were visiting the Bernards at their home for dinner, Monsieur Bernard turned to Inge with a smile and said, "Inge, say something in Swedish."

Inge saw Moc's face turn ashen. *Was Monsieur Bernard suspicious? Had she given herself away?* Her Swedish accent was probably not very good, but how could she know? How would *anyone* know? Maybe he was a Greta Garbo fan. With clammy hands and a trembling chin, but without skipping a beat, she picked up her glass and exclaimed, *"Skoal"*—the only Swedish word she knew. Everyone else raised their glasses and joined in: "Skoal!" Later, Moc wondered what would have happened if the Bernards had invited Swedish acquaintances.

This event forced Inge to think about what it meant to be German. It didn't feel right to hide who she was, but she also didn't feel she was responsible for what the Germans had done. She realized that times were changing, and that the world—and she—needed to come to terms with Germany's actions during the war. Soon, two parallel events would combine to crystallize Inge's further thoughts.

The first happened just a few days later. As they were out and about, Inge and Moc spotted an elegant gentleman walking along the street. Moc could't believe it. "Inge, look. That's Mr. Teal, the American I worked for in Marburg." Mr. Teal recognized Moc too and rushed to embrace him. "Mr. Teal! What are you doing in Paris? Why didn't you go back to America?"

A slow smile crossed Mr. Teal's face. "Oh, Moc, it's a long story. Why don't you and Inge come over to my apartment and meet my wife? I can tell you all about it. I'm sure you have some stories to tell, too."

Inge had spent little time with Americans and was looking forward to meeting them. They had made many new friends in Paris, but it would also be nice to see someone from the "old times." When they arrived at the apartment, their hosts welcomed them graciously. Mr. Teal said, "Well, I think now you can now call me by my given name, Gert. I want you to meet my wife, Sophie."

Sophie warmly embraced Inge and said, "Come into the kitchen and help me with dinner. I am making *hutspot met klapstuk.*

Inge recognized the dish and found it curious because she knew it as a traditional Dutch meal, not American. "Are you Dutch?" she asked.

"Yes. We're temporally in Paris for Gert's job, but our home is in Amsterdam. Come and visit us."

The four sat in the dining room and enjoyed the roast with mashed potatoes and carrots. After the main course, and with the small talk out of the way, Gert began to share his story. "Moc, there are things you didn't know at the time when we met in Marburg. I am actually not American at all. I'm Dutch, and with the Dutch resistance I worked with the American Office of Strategic Services as the war was ending. Our job was to remove Nazi influence from German life by liquidating the Nazi Party and bringing the guilty to justice."

Inge was overwhelmed by the thought that Gert had placed his life on the line to resist the Nazis. Every day, for years, he put himself at risk of death to defend his country and foil the invaders. The *Germans*. And yet he had befriended Inge and Moc, helped them in any way that he could, and even welcomed them into his home. Inge thought, *Here is a man who did all that he could, even in the face of mortal danger. What would I have done in those circumstances?*

The second event was a piece of mail. Moc handed the envelope to Inge and said, "You have a letter from Germany that is not from your parents."

Inge was curious. "Who would write to me?" She opened it with delight to find it was from Ingeline, her childhood friend from Königsberg. Ingeline had found Inge's parents and got Inge's address from them.

In the letter, Ingeline said she was divorced and had a child. The two friends hadn't seen each other since Ingeline left to study in England after they both finished school. Ingeline was eager to come visit Inge in Paris and rekindle their connection, and Inge couldn't wait to see her.

Soon the visit was planned. Ingeline would come alone without her daughter who was being cared for by her father. She confessed that her relationship with her child wasn't good. When Inge arrived at the train station she felt a sting in her heart. The childhood friends were now both adults and their life experiences had forged two different paths. This weekend together would allow them to reconnect. Moc would be working all weekend, allowing the two old friends to be young girls together again.

Ingeline stepped off the train. She had grown into a tall woman who seemed to embrace her height with confidence. Her face ignited into a smile and her eyes glistened with joyful tears when she saw Inge. "How many years has it been? I can't believe we are together again. It must be at least sixteen years. So much has happened." Their arms entwined as they began the long walk to Inge's apartment. A feast of their favorite pastries and coffee was ready for them when they arrived.

Although years had passed, their love for one another hadn't diminished in the slightest. Each looked at the other, aware of the imprint that the years had left. Like old times, they took pastries and coffee and snuggled in Inge's bed to share confidences.

Ingeline said, "I was studying in England but had to return to Germany when England declared war. You had left by then; we just missed each other. I felt alone coming back to Königsberg, and the city no longer felt like home. My darling father was distant and clearly preoccupied. He paid little attention to my return." Inge could see the anguish sketched on her face as her lips tightened and her breathing shallowed. "I was so alone and I searched for connection with someone, anyone. I quickly found Dieter. He was a German officer about to go fight in Poland. We married quickly against my father's wishes. Maybe it was my way of getting back at him. To my surprise, I quickly became pregnant and those nine months were unimaginable misery." Inge knew that any movement, any sound, would deter Ingeline from continuing. She was immobilized by her story and the pain that emanated from her friend.

Ingeline slowly continued. "Dieter was wounded in Poland. He lost his right arm. He was sent home broken. But that wasn't the worst thing that happened." A long silence fell on the two friends. Inge waited, anchored in place. "As I think about our time together, I am awed by how naïve we were. You and I lived our lives totally unaware of what was happening around us. We were completely politically unaware." Inge felt pangs of guilt reflecting on her own obliviousness. "I don't know how much you remember my father. He was always working. He brought in alcohol and spirits to Königsberg from the West. Unlike us, he was politically active. He told me to be careful when I spoke on the phone. I thought he was silly, but now I know he was worried someone was listening. He never told me he was part of the German resistance. It was really only a small band of East Prussian men trying to engage in subversion and conspiracy. They were such a small group that I don't think they had any success." Ingeline stopped to catch her breath. Her chin lowered to her chest with soft sobs. "My mother said at ten o'clock one night a customer of my father's knocked at the door. He was a tiny man who felt important because he was wearing a Nazi uniform. But he apparently liked my father and was warning him. He said, 'I just want to let you know we know about your associations and they are coming to arrest you in the morning.'" Inge wanted to cover her ears. She could only imagine what followed. "My father went into the basement and shot himself that night. I was three months pregnant at the time. I know the shock affected me deeply and interfered with the pregnancy. I was overwhelmed with grief. It was all I knew. My grief prevented me from connecting with my daughter, and it was my grief that ruined my relationship with my husband. I've never been the same."

    Inge realized how little she understood her friend's suffering. The sadness permeated her body and made her queasy. The nausea continued for weeks. Inge had been deeply impacted by Ingeline's story, but she really thought she should be feeling better.

By this time she and Moc were married nine years, and their attempts to have children had been fruitless. The idea that she might be pregnant hadn't even occurred to her. *Could she be?*

On a rainy Wednesday, Inge made arrangements to leave work early and stop at the doctor just to rule out the possibility. When she heard the results, she took a moment to grasp the reality. Many times she had wished to hear that she would be a mother; she was still unprepared for the effect that the words had upon her. She was elated and radiantly happy. She was also nervous, worried, and afraid. She set about planning her announcement, heart beating rapidly, as she walked along the rain-slickened streets. When she got home she would smile and hang up her coat, leaving her umbrella in the front hall to dry. She would sit on the settee and pat the cushion, inviting Moc to join her. She would ask him to guess what amazing thing had happened to her today. And when he gave up, she would tell him the wonderful news. She imagined his reaction, his smiles and tears, even as she felt a sort of panic creeping into her thoughts, subverting her happiness. What was it? Everything had changed in an instant; in the blink of an eye she was no longer just Inge, the fun, fashionable, carefree girl that she had always imagined herself to be. In truth, she knew that it had been years since she'd been that girl, but only now did she see herself as something more, a new person, a woman with responsibilities that stretched far beyond her own welfare. And it worried her.

When she arrived at the apartment, Moc was already there, just as she had expected. He waved his newspaper in greeting and all of Inge's carefully laid plans went out the window. She simply blurted, "We're going to have a baby," and waited for his reply.

At first he was silent, expressionless. For an instant Inge feared that he was angry. But, just like her, he needed a moment to absorb her words and sort out the thousands of thoughts that dashed through his head. Finally, his mouth spread into a big smile and he took her up in his arms and spun her around. Still holding her close, he looked into her eyes, overwhelmed by his love, pride, and affection for Inge, the woman with whom he had shared so much. "I love you, Inge. And this changes everything. I'll find a way to make more money. You won't have to work anymore; you have more important things to take care of. We need a better place to live. This apartment is fine for the two of us, but for a family? It isn't enough. There are so many things to do, and I know I'll think of more things every day, but we have to get started. And can you imagine? We'll be raising our child in *Paris*."

Inge collapsed into the settee. Moc was happy. She was glad for that. And she was happy. She knew that she was. Why didn't she *feel* happy? The nagging worry continued to eat at her thoughts. What was it? *Can you imagine? We'll be raising our child in Paris*. Everything came into focus, and the words seemed to pass her lips without conscious thought. "I don't want to stay in Paris."

Moc was stunned. "Why not? We are among the luckiest people in the world. We came through the war, both of us, in better shape than most. Here we are in one of the world's greatest cities. The potential is limitless. People everywhere dream of living here. We actually get to do it. Aren't you happy? Why would we leave?"

"I love Paris, too. And I am happy, but I'm happy with *you*. We've become comfortable here. Even if we get new jobs and move to a new apartment, we're still doing what's easy. It's tempting, it's reassuring, but it isn't really living. Years ago, I promised myself that I would live an extraordinary life. I feel like, with all we've been through, we've been given an opportunity to do that." She took Moc's hand and squeezed it. "I want to go to Mexico. I want to see places I've never seen, and be among people I've never met, and learn a new language, and be someone who knows what it's like to really experience all that the world has to offer. And I can't do that from an apartment in Paris. I want to live the life that I promised myself and I want to do it with you."

Moc smiled and brushed the hair away from her face. She could tell that he wasn't entirely convinced, but he would come around. "You're right," he said. "We'll have the baby here in Paris, then we'll go to Mexico. After all, that's what we planned to do to begin with, wasn't it? It's surprising how quickly we're willing to let things go when we get settled and fall into a routine. And after Mexico, who knows? Maybe we'll go to the US and attend glamorous house parties with famous Hollywood stars."

Inge laughed. Moc wrapped his arm around her and she relaxed into his embrace. She thought of all they'd been through and the people they'd met along the way, and she thought of all that was yet to come. This was the beginning of a bold new adventure. *I will live an extraordinary life,* she thought to herself. Inge placed a hand on her belly and imagined the life growing within her. *And you will live an extraordinary life as well.*

German newspaper featuring story (see picture and caption on facing page) about young German couple living in Paris.

Pierre Arbelle's fashionable letterhead

> „Die persönliche Freiheit hier ist wunderbar!" Ernst Krumm-Heller, Physiologe aus Marburg, lebt mit seiner Frau seit sechs Jahren in Paris. Er wollte damals eigentlich nach Mexiko auswandern, mußte in Paris auf verschiedene Papiere warten, und zufällig bot sich ihm die Gelegenheit, in einem pharmazeutischen Betrieb Laborchef zu werden. Er verdient über 1200 D-Mark und ist an verschiedenen Präparaten finanziell beteiligt. Seine Frau und er machen ab und zu einen Besuch in Deutschland, aber ganz wollen sie nicht mehr zurück. Einzige Klage: das Wohnen! Sie beide haben Jahre hindurch im Hotel gewohnt, bis sie endlich die Möglichkeit hatten, eine kleine bescheidene Wohnung zu beziehen.

Translation: *The individual freedom here is great! Krumm-Heller, a physiologist from Marburg and his wife have lived in Paris for six years. He actually wanted to emigrate to Mexico but had to wait in Paris for various paper. By coincidence he was given the opportunity to work at a pharmaceutical laboratory and earn over 1200 Deutch and had other financial prospects. He and his wife visit Germany on occasion but don't really want to return. The only complaint has been the living arrangements. For years they both had to live in a hotel until they had the means to buy a small apartment.*

Inge and Moc in Paris

Inge's Jewelry. 1. Henri's ring 2. Moc's mother garnet broach 3. Moc's mother's ring designed by his father 4. Pearl and diamond earrings Inge got on her birthday 5. ½ gold coin left over from wedding rings

Ingeline, Inge's childhood friend

Epilogue

To My Inès,

Today you celebrate your 50^h birthday—Happy Birthday—half a century. Quite a milestone and we have come a long way—from Paris to Mexico to the Good Old USA. Along the way we have had good times and bad times. The worst time was when we lost your Papi. He was still so young. He missed out on seeing you grow-up. To see you today, the woman you became—on the way to become a Ph.D. But, I know he walked with you along the way. I am sure of that. He will be so pleased at what he sees.

As for me—I thank God every day for you. You are the best daughter a mother can wish for. You never gave me any trouble. Your accomplishments make me proud. I am glad you had the support to accomplish your dream

The first 50 have been good to you. I hope the next 50 years will be as good. I will always be with you and watch over you wherever I may be.

I love you,
Mami

THE LETTER MY MOTHER wrote to me on my fiftieth birthday affected me deeply. Reading it now, a few years after her death, feels like she is reaching back to me and watching over me on this project of sharing the stories of her life. I believe she wanted her story told. Her life spanned an era of transformative history, and her experiences during the war transformed her, too. She grew from a naïve teenager to a woman of dimension, grateful for a fortunate path. In one conversation with a friend, I overheard her say, "My philosophy of life has always been positive. I have never allowed myself to get stuck in darkness and depression, but rather take life as it comes."

While cleaning out her home after she died, I found some old boxes stacked deep in the closet. One was a shoebox containing time-worn 8mm reels. I knew instantly what they were, but I didn't know she had kept them. My mind stumbled back to my childhood, remembering the excitement of receiving the movie camera under the Christmas tree when I was eleven. I took the reels from the box and sent them away to be transferred to DVDs. When I received the discs, I put one in the machine and held my breath.

It was our last family vacation. The grainy images sparked the memory of the morning we left for Acapulco, and it was as if I were there again, in the moment. We squeeze into my father's white Chrysler, with its scratched red roof, for the five-hour drive. My mother smiles regally, elegant as always, with her ever-present cigarette. Father, with his white shirt and bright smile, waves at the camera. My shoulder-length blond hair is combed into a *flip,* the movie star's style of the day, and I'm wearing a red gingham blouse, which like so many of my clothes did little to camouflage my childhood plumpness. Friends from the United States were visiting. They were not relatives, but I called him Tante Lony and Onkle Hank.

This small band of travelers headed off to an Acapulco adventure. We stopped midway to look at the scenery below us. I don't remember appreciating the breathtaking view; I was too eager to get to our beach destination. However, the adults were awestruck by the ocean and the surrounding mountains. It was Tante Lony's and Onkle Hank's first trip to Acapulco, and they wanted to take in the full experience.

The family scheduled a glass-bottomed boat to a remote island in the Acapulco gulf known as Isla de La Roqueta, the legendary home of hidden pirate treasure. I remember having visions of digging in the sand and finding it.

The predicted weather was a warm eighty-eight degrees with no rain, since January is the dry season in Mexico. I was not agile, so getting into the boat was difficult. The boat was white with peeling paint and hardly seemed seaworthy. It had a blue torn canvas roof that protected us from the sun, but not from the pungent smell of fish. We sat on rickety benches, and I saw yellow life vests on board that, even at eleven years old, I knew was a good thing. Nonetheless, I refused to wear one.

I sat between Tante Lony and my mother. My father and Onkle Hank sat in the front. The ride to the island took about thirty minutes. I looked through dirty opaque glass panels on the bottom of the boat and saw the fish and the rocky sea bottom. But even in my imagination, I couldn't see any treasure.

When we arrived at Isla de La Roqueta, we clumsily disembarked. We set up our vantage point close to the water and slathered on the sunblock. I watched my father put the sunscreen on my mother's back, and she put the sticky white cream all over me, especially my face because I burned so easily. Well protected, I set out to explore the island. I was careful not to venture too far and made sure I always kept in sight of my family. Once I determined that the treasure was not in the immediate vicinity, I waded into the water.

On the 8mm footage from that day, there is an image of my back, dressed in my bright yellow bathing suit, creeping through the waves. I see myself looking around and have a memory of the plan I was crafting. I could see the other shore across Acapulco Bay. I wasn't a strong swimmer, but I was determined to swim across and reach the other shore. I set out and kept stroking until my arms reached exhaustion. I realized that I would not reach my goal and sadly turned around and swim back to the island. What I didn't know was that my parents on the shore became concerned about my recklessness and that my father came in after me. We both returned to shore exhausted.

After my failed adventure in the ocean, I was famished and devoured the picnic lunch the hotel had prepared. There were ham sandwiches and fruit; the juicy red apple invigorated me. After lunch, I dug in the sand, still looking for the treasure. I watched my mother lazily sunning herself in the hot sun, chatting with Tante Lony and Onkle Hank who was engrossed in his book. I saw my father heading for the waves, but after my misadventure in the water, I was not too eager to join him and get wet again.

After a brief swim, my father returned to the shore. We could tell something was wrong with him. He was pale and staggered halfway across the sand before he collapsed. I saw the panic in my mother's face. Although Isla de La Roqueta was remote, they still had rudimentary first aid. A quasi-paramedic unit rushed to my father and carried him to a makeshift ambulance boat to take him to the Acapulco hospital. My mother and Onkle Hank went with him. Tante Lony stayed behind with me to take a later boat.

I didn't fully understand the implications of what had happened. I knew enough to be frightened, and I knew enough to worry about what was to come. Tante Lony and I boarded the return boat, but this time the ride was different. I wasn't at all interested in the fish or in any hidden treasure. I clung to Tante Lony. Although I said nothing, I worried that my reckless attempt to swim to the other shore had caused my father's over-exertion and made him get sick. Since I told no one of my fear, there was no one to allay my guilt.

When we returned to the hotel, there was still no word from my mother and Onkle Hank. Tante Lony helped me get ready for bed. She was kind and caring and kept trying to assure me that everything would be okay. But even at eleven years old I could see the doubt in her eyes. Despite my fears and worries, I must have fallen asleep, alone in the room I shared with my parents. I woke when my mother walked into the room. The words she spoke still ring in my ear today. *"Papi ist tot."* My father was dead.

It is often said that life can change in the blink of an eye. Ours did. Suddenly my mother and I were alone. We had friends in Mexico, but staying there didn't seem like a viable option. Unkle Hank and Tante Lony suggested that we start new lives in America. My mother had started a new life several times over. This would be her next opportunity to recreate herself. She had achieved quiet acceptance of life in Paris and then changed the architecture of her life by moving to Mexico. The move to America was a new blueprint for the future.

Paralleling my mother's life transitions, the move to America became my juncture point. It altered the flow of my life. I was a twelve-year-old transplant from Mexico to the foreign land of mid-sixties American teenagerhood. Life in the US was very different from Mexico. I was amazed at the freedom and independence teenagers were allowed. It was a total departure from the sheltered lifestyle of my childhood. The contrast allowed me to push the edge of possibilities. I became the quintessential American youth. Experiences that I never could have imagined in Mexico, such as riding a bicycle in the street or playing kickball in the schoolyard, became elements of my daily life.

It's difficult to pull apart the elements of identity. Looking deeply into ourselves involves the willingness to peel back layers. The perpetual question of nature vs nurture is an inevitable quandary. How much of who I am is forged in the story of my parents, how much was contributed by my own experiences, and how much was designated by the genes that were passed on to me? I remember my mother and see pictures of her at the age I am today. We look alike in many ways. Without intent, however, my hair is arranged in a similar way and the clothes I choose have an identical flair. I have the same yearning for fashion and elegance that she did. But from a different reservoir, I became the heir of my father's single-minded pursuit of goals.

As I piece together the web of memories from my life I create perspective and understand how the shifting sands in my parent's lives set me on a similar path. I, too, began a life of evolving transitions and adaptations. Without the same backdrop as theirs, my travels took me to many US states, Panama, and El Salvador. My travels were courtesy of my husband's military assignments but, like my mother, with each move I had to readjust, revise, and reinvent my identity in order to acclimate to my surroundings.

Life's adaptations are expressed in a metaphor by

Ruthellen Josselson writing about identity in *Revising Herself: The Story of a Woman's Identity from College to Midlife*: "Like a slowly turning kaleidoscope, the shifts in a woman's identity involve rearrangements of pieces, now accenting one aspect and muting another, now altering the arrangement once more." The kaleidoscope of my mother's life and my own brought us to colors and images that we bequeath to the cycle of generations that follow us.

I hope that the story of my mother's life provides a plumb line for her grandchildren and great-grandchildren. As long as someone remembers your life, your legacy will live on. This story provides the means to remember Inge and her life and allow her legacy to echo in the lives of future generations.

Scan the QR code or visit https://tinyurl.com/smy897j *to see the original 8mm film from Acapulco.*

Acknowledgments

WRITING CAN BE A lonely pursuit. A strong support system provides encouragement to keep going. I am grateful that my circle of support has been the scaffolding allowing me to fulfill my vision of converting my mother's life story into a book.

I am thankful to my dearest friend, Dr. Susan Goldberg. She has been with me since the inception of this goal. She used her skills and extraordinary empathy to conduct the narrative interview with my mother. Therefore, she knows the stories from the inside and helped me shape my thoughts and my writing. I always reached out to her when I became discouraged. I counted on her to provide the motivation the propelled me forward. I could not have done it without her, and I will be eternally grateful for her friendship.

Researching and writing about our ancestors has become a popular pursuit. Lynn Palermo's Family History Writing Studio helps family historians transform their research into shareable stories. I learned a great deal about writing by participating in Lynn's workshops. I am also grateful to Lynn's Inner Circle group for providing valuable feedback on my writing and suggestions on how to improve.

The collaboration with my editor, Jason Liller of Liller Creative LLC, provided the partnership that I needed to forge the path to completing the writing of my mother's story. Jason became my sounding board, and my cheerleader as he fostered my growth as a writer. His keen eye, attention to detail, and "onward" philosophy kept me moving forward. It is an odd statement for a writer to say, but words fail me in capturing just the immense sense of gratitude I feel towards Jason. I know he put in tireless hours in shaping and polishing my writing. I know deep in my core that the book would not have been a reality without his professionalism and dedication to my vision.

I am filled with gratitude for my husband, Carl. His loving support has allowed me to fulfill all of my dreams and to follow whatever path I set my sights on. His discerning eye has been a guiding post fueling my inspiration, and it has been my immense pleasure to share my life journey with him. Thank you.

About the Author

DR. INES KRUMM-HELLER ROE is a psychologist who believes that we all have a story to tell. Hers begins with growing up in Mexico and, as an eleven-year-old fluent in German and Spanish, emigrating to the US. She often jokes that she learned English by watching 1960s TV shows and reading Nancy Drew books. The wife of a service member, she lived at military posts throughout the US and returned to Latin America when her husband was stationed in Panama and El Salvador. Today, Dr. Roe lives in Pennsylvania where she provides psychological services, helping her patients navigate their life struggles and shape their own stories.

www.ingramcontent.com/pod-product-compliance
Lightning Source LLC
Chambersburg PA
CBHW061655040426
42446CB00010B/1750